Self Portrait: An Artist's Memories

To Gregory
Mark and
Natalia

Best wishes

Madam Alexander
(Sacha)

Self Portrait:
An Artist's Memories

Nadine Alexandre

CREATIVE ARTS BOOK COMPANY
Berkeley, California

For information contact:
Creative Arts Book Company
833 Bancroft Way
Berkeley, California 94710

ISBN 0-88739-330-6
Library of Congress Catalog Number 99-069767

This book is dedicated to the memories of my beloved mother Lola, my father Alexander, and my brother Albert, Holocaust martyrs; and to the memory of my cherished granddaughter Ashley, whom the Lord took at the age of twenty months.

Prologue

In 1991, in a tragic accident, my only son lost his beloved little girl. I was disconsolate, sick with grief, and mourned her death for over a year. Then one day I took a pen and jotted down a few lines, going very far back in my memory. I wrote about the Holocaust, which took my parents and brother, and about my life in Paris during the Nazi occupation. I wrote to escape my great pain. As a healing form of therapy, this manuscript was born.

Self Portrait: An Artist's Memories

Chapter One

MY FIRST RECOLLECTION of childhood is when I was about four years old. We lived in a basement room on a bleak street called Rue Pia, opposite a sloping vacant lot. My father, a scholar, was born in Vilno, Lithuania. On a trip to Warsaw, Poland, he met the woman who was to be my mother. They married, and soon I was born. They immigrated to France and settled in Paris, where another child was born, a baby boy. The four of us lived in a one-room basement.

I remember going to play in the vacant lot across the street. There were some young boys, seven or eight years old. One of the boys, the biggest one, grabbed me and threatened to throw me down the slope if I didn't pull my pants down. I ran home screaming. It was a rough neighborhood, full of thieves and hoodlums.

We soon moved to a district of Paris that was predominantly Jewish, a little ghetto called Belleville. The apartment building we moved into was gray and dismal. It was on Rue Bisson, a rather narrow street. On the other side of the street was a Bain-Douche, where one could take baths or showers. In the days before the war there were communal baths. On the same street were several shops. Merchants had kegs of wine outside their doors, and barrels of fish and pickles were displayed outside grocery stores. Rock-sugar candy on a string was only a sou.

We lived in one medium-sized room with a kitchen. It had one window facing a courtyard. We were on the third floor. There was an elevator, like a cage. The bathroom at the end of the hall consisted of a hole in the concrete floor, with two marks to set one's feet. The toilet paper, usually newspaper cut into medium sized squares, hung by a string near the door, which had no locks but did have a peep hole.

The room was sparsely furnished with a large bed for my parents, a small bed against the wall, a folded cot in one corner, a table, and some chairs. An armoire with an oval mirror was at the far end of the room. On the wall near the door two family portraits hung in faded gilded frames. The kitchen had a red tile floor, a large iron stove, and in the opposite corner a small gas range with two burners, where my mother would cook most of our meals. Coal and wood were scarce in those pre-war years.

I recall going with my mother and brother to a parc called Butte Chaumont, sitting on a bench and eating hot stew out of a pot. Mother didn't believe in taking shortcuts and would rather burden herself by carrying along her cooking implements. It was her old-fashioned way. I went to a nearby girls' school, and my brother went to a boys' school. Geography, literature, and history were my favorite subjects but I was only mediocre in mathematics.

I was seven years old when my younger brother was born. He was the most beautiful child I had ever seen; my maternal instincts awoke very early. He was a blond, blue-eyed boy named Andre, but I quickly nicknamed him Dédé. I would care for Dédé, as I loved him dearly. As a child, I never owned a doll, but my father gave me a set of colored crayons when I was six.

I was an avid reader, and by age nine, I had read George Sand, de Maupassant, Lamartine, and Balzac. I had made friends with two spinster ladies whose apartment I could see across from our window. They often invited me to their crowded room where I found many books. The books were my companions; I became a voracious reader.

I seldom saw my father, but on one occasion when I was a tiny girl, I recall he took me for a walk on the icy streets of Paris in the winter. I fell on the ice. To console me, he took me to a restaurant where it was warm. I noticed people there knew him and liked him. Everyone spoke Yiddish.

My mother loved the theater. She had been a ballet dancer in her younger days in Poland. We went out once to a music hall on Rue de Belleville. There were several vaudeville acts and I enjoyed that outing very much. We also went to the movies and I remember the theater on Rue de Belleville where I saw my first movie, *Gunga Din*.

My father was a leather glove cutter and worked in a small factory. Sometimes he would bring some work home and cut gloves on a makeshift table in our kitchen. I used to watch him as he designed the gloves artfully. I sat on the floor and tried to imitate him, drawing the outline of my hand.

War started! They were rounding up men everywhere. Our neighbors warned my father that buses going through our street were full of men being sent to camps. One day my father went out to get a pack of cigarettes and

"PARC BUTTES-CHAUMONT"

Sitting on a bench and
eating out of a "casserole"
Hot stew, mother would
give us lunch, DURING WAR
in FRANCE!

3

my father was a leather glove cutter
I sat on the floor and tried to imitate him
drawing the outline of my hand.

never returned. In 1941, Mother had a photo taken of us three children and herself to send to Father at the camp. We never knew if he received it, for we weren't sure in which concentration camp he was imprisoned. Many years later I learned he was sent to Drancy and from there to Auschwitz to the gas chambers, along with thousands of other people.

For a year we struggled to survive in our small Paris apartment. My mother had no money, no income; we were very poor. I remember her keeping our place clean and neatly scrubbed. She saved bread every day that she would put between clean sheets in the armoire. The small baguettes were first white, then gray, then grayer, as the bakers mixed sawdust and other unknown ingredients in the bread during those bleak days.

The air raids continued in Paris, and I recall going to cellars with our gas masks and blankets. That summer of 1941, the city air was suffocating, and the skies were gray with smoke. Mother sent Dédé and me to a farm in the country run by peasants through an organization that helped single mothers send their children away from the dangers of Paris. The farm was dreary and I was lonesome for my mother and brother, but I looked after Dédé and we had food to eat.

One rainy day Mother came to see us. I kissed her and felt the warmth of her bosom. Then, as I watched through the fence, she left in the rain. I thought then that I might never see her again and I shivered at that premonition. I was ten years old and very much alone, except for my little brother.

When we returned to Paris, we learned that hundreds of families had been rounded up, like cattle, in the ghetto of Belleville. Women and children were sent to the infamous Vel D'Hiv, and from there to concentration camps. My mother and brother were among them. They were sent to the gas chambers at Auschwitz in 1942. Mother was thirty years old. My brother was nine.

By some miracle Dédé and I were still together. We were sheltered in various places. At one time a prostitute kept us in one room as she was doing business in another. I heard German voices through the walls and knew she was entertaining Gestapo. Dédé and I were forced to move to different places all the time, since we were hiding from the SS. Dédé was four years old, a sweet, beautiful boy.

I recall one place in particular, located in a very poor district of Paris. A woman named Madame Irma took us in. She was Christian, but her husband, Monsieur Leon, was Jewish, and in hiding from the Germans. Madame Irma had a young retarded son, who was constantly in convulsions and drooling most of the time in his small bed. Monsieur Leon was a bookseller by trade. In their small but neat apartment, I found many books to read: Pierre Loti,

At one time a prostitute
non descript in appearance, kept us
in one room as she was doing busness
in another, I heard German voices and
knew she was entertaining Gestapo.

Verlaine, Pierre Louys, Rimbaud. Those books fascinated me much at the time. Madame Irma was a good soul. She had known my parents and had heard from witnesses that, during the roundup of women and children on our street, my mother had gotten on her knees on the rough cobblestones and prayed that my little brother and I would be safe. I cried a lot when Madame Irma told me this. She then shoved in my hand some crumpled photographs. Among them was the photo we four had taken together to send to my father in the camps, and a small ring with a red stone in it. They were the only things she could salvage from our little home. A family had lived in that small apartment.

During the German occupation, many underground groups were organized to save as many children as possible. We were among the more than one hundred children that were regrouped and sent to a large house for disinfecting. It was on Rue Lamarck in Paris. Here they set up a dormitory and every one of us had our heads shaved. We wore striped pajamas. We were very thin. I remember holding my little brother's hand tightly. We had only one meal a day and we were afraid. We were there only a short time, when one night some men and women came in and took several of children to a waiting truck. Dédé and I were among the chosen children. Unbeknownst to us at the time, that house was a place designated by the Gestapo for children who were being sent to concentration camps. That is what happened the very next day to all the rest of the children, who were rounded up and loaded into cattle trains.

Dédé and I were taken to other hidden safe houses. I did manage to finish school early and earned a "certificate D'Etudes," while my little brother and I were living with a nice family in the suburbs of Paris, in a town called Aulnay S/Bois. It was there that the news of the liberation came. The war was over!

Once more, we children were regrouped at a large children's home on the outskirts of Paris, a place called St. Cloud, where we stayed a short while. From there I was sent with a group of boys and girls to a facility called Malmaison, while Dédé was sent nearby to a house called Vieux Phare. Malmaison was very pleasant, near a chateau. The main house had about fifteen rooms, a dining hall, kitchen, a green area or parc, and a small vegetable garden. We were nine or ten girls to about thirty boys. We girls had our dormitory at the end of the parc, a large room with many windows, and I remember when I first entered it, I smelled the odor of paint thinner. It could have been an artist's former studio. Soon small beds arrived for each of us girls, aged thirteen to fifteen years old.

The woman who ran our home was a kind lady doctor who made us girls feel special. At Malmaison we lived in what could be called a commune; everyone had daily chores, kitchen duty, garden duty, laundry, and so forth. There was good camaraderie among all of us. Boys and girls mingled together at play and chores. The boys were protective of us girls, as we were younger and in the minority.

Most of the girls were sent to vocational schools to learn sewing and homemaking. When I was asked what I wanted to study, as I had rebelled against going to sewing classes, I said I wanted to study art. I was sent to an art school to learn fashion design and drawing. My first school was in Montparnasse, a district known for its artistic and Bohemian life. It was about ten kilometers from the orphanage of Malmaison and I had to take an early bus every morning. In the post-war years, I went to classes and participated in life at Malmaison.

A man arrived soon in our midst and we learned that he was sent to indoctrinate us for life in Israel, then a new state, and to teach us the Hebrew language, to prepare us for living in a kibbutz. Many of the children did emigrate to Israel.

Through some distant contacts from the Paris ghetto, I had met a French Jewish lawyer and his wife, whose sister and brother-in-law lived in New York and wanted to adopt a war-orphaned boy. They saw photos of Dédé who was then nine years old and such a sweet child. The response from the couple, the Hosbergs, was immediate. They sent for Dédé and he sailed for New York on the Queen Mary in 1946.

The separation was almost unbearable for me, but I understood that he would have a chance for a new life, a home and parents to care for and love him, and a new country in which to grow up and become a man. I was not to see my little brother again for almost ten years.

Israel was not for me; I did not want to be indoctrinated. The children at Malmaison dispersed: some to Israel, others to new homes, and I too left, at age sixteen. Some kind friends found me a maid's room in the district of Passy in Paris. I was given a small allowance to help me out in the beginning and a few clothes, but I was healthy, young, and full of the anticipation of life.

That winter was bitterly cold. I had shoes with wooden soles, and a coat made from an old horse blanket. It reminded me of an incident during the German occupation, when each Jew was required to wear the yellow Star of David on his or her coat. While walking down the long Metro corridor I had heard footsteps behind me. Two German soldiers were running. Fortunately as they ran past me, I held my arm tightly to hide the yellow star.

The first time I had seen American soldiers was when they marched into Paris along the Champs Elysées on Liberation Day. I was fifteen years old at the time and, as other young girls, was fascinated by these good-looking and generous young men. We loved their music, especially their jazz, and it was then that I heard for the first time the famous "In the Mood." Paris was full of Americans in those post-war years. Many G.I.s were studying in Paris at various universities, and a large number of soldiers came on leave from occupied Germany. A popular bar called The Vikings was on the same narrow street where my school was located in Montparnasse. I began to stop there often and always found a group of American students. I practiced my English with these students at the Vikings, and also at the Café des Etats Unis on Boulevard Raspail in Montparnasse. A group of us would often take our meals at Wajda, where the owner would accept as payment some of our artwork, which decorated the walls of the restaurant. Many famous painters ate there. The Quartier Latin was another of my favorite places. The Dupont Café on the Boulevard St. Michel was always full of students. La rue du chat qui Pêche was the narrowest street in Paris.

Near the Sorbonne and behind the Pantheon were many exotic, ethnic places, cafés, and restaurants where you could eat African, Asiatic, Burmese, Greek, or Italian food and hear music of all sorts. The many boites were good places to meet young friends. The Quais de la Seine by the river was a fascinating place to me, as were the people who walked by the many bookstalls and booksellers. My first dance party was in a crowded bourgeois apartment, on the top floor of the building. I was wearing a light dress, as it was spring. A good-looking young man, Lionel, asked me to dance and to a rendezvous in the Bois de Boulogne the next day for a picnic. Lionel had blond hair and a gentle smile. I thought I had fallen in love, but I never saw him again.

I went to the Louvre Museum to copy the masters. One, a particularly mystical painting by Gericauld, held me entranced. It was "The Raft of the Meduse," a powerful study, a great masterpiece. While I liked the classic art, I was very moved when I saw the wheat fields and black birds by Vincent Van Gogh and I loved the colors of Monet. I was a good draftsman and very adept with charcoal. Once my anatomy teacher asked us to draw a picture of our own foot. I did an excellent rendering of mine and was commended for it.

I was a Paris wanderer and I remember walking on a crowded boulevard in the popular district of Reaumur-Sebastopol. As the crowd passed by, with men looking at me, at my full figure, slender waist and bouncy breasts, my

in Montparnasse
"Wadja" where the owner would accept
as payment some of our art work which
decorated the walls of the restaurant

eyes caught the attention of a man who was demonstrating a culinary gadget in front of a store. In my innocence, I accepted when he asked me if I would like to eat dinner at his place. We walked up a dingy flight of stairs. I was only looking for a hot meal, as my diet at that time consisted of cornet of frites and sandwiches. We arrived in his small room. As the man was waiting for the pork chops to be cooked, he suddenly grabbed me, forced me down on the bed, and tried to unbutton my blouse. In reflex, I took the top of the petrol lamp and threatened to hit him with it. While he backed away, I ran as fast as I could down the smelly stairs into the street. My stomach was empty lots of times.

I took pleasure in going to the cinema and would favor American films. I saw *Blue Skies* four or five times in a cinema on the Champs Elysées. Saint Germain des Prés was also one of my favorite places, where one could sit in a café for hours, and dream and talk for only the price of a café crème. I remember La Pergola, La Reine Blanche, and the famous Deux Magots, home of Jean Paul Sartre and other existentialists of that period. The Mabillon was an unpretentious café on the Boulevard St. Germain. I used to sit there very often until four in the morning with my sketchpad on my lap, a plate of cheese and pears in front of me. In those days many cafés in Paris were open all night. After leaving the Mabillon, I went across the Boulevard to La Pergola, where one could eat a good onion soup gratiné. The place was usually filled at that time of morning with intellectuals, pseudo-intellectuals, pimps, prostitutes, students, and artists. It was a lively place! Then upon the closing of La Pergola at six o'clock in the morning, I usually went to the first café open early for the workers and the street cleaners, drinking their first vin rouge of the morning. After I drank a last café crème I went to my room to sleep a few hours before going to art classes with live models at the Academie de la Grande Chaumiere, in Montparnasse.

As I was walking in Paris, climbing the steep narrow streets and stairs of Montmartre, I would often sit under the shade of the trees in the provincial little places surrounding Montmartre. In the evening, for a few francs, I would sketch people dining in restaurants in the open air and cafés. On top of the hill near the Church of the Sacre Coeur was a square filled with tables where people dined in the evenings and the young artists could be seen painting their impressions of the picturesque district.

I had now deserted Montparnasse for St Germain des Prés, which had more of a quaint village atmosphere and from which my living quarters were only twenty minutes by Metro. I remember going to my first discotheque on

Living in Saint
Germain
after WW II.

LA MÈRE CATHERINE

Montmartre

Boulevard St Germain. A dark room, a record player and a few young people dancing; I was unimpressed. What I liked in those days was going to popular dancing halls, like the one near Pigalle, where one could see the glass ball in the ceiling, reflecting the young couples dancing to slow fox trots, tangos and waltzes. The place was called le Tahiti, a very evocative name. On the grand boulevards was another popular dance hall for shop girls and young workmen. It was there that I first learned to boogie. At the always crowded and very famous Cave, called la Rose Rouge, you would find a pulsating jazz by Claude Luter, King of Dixie. Juliette Greco was the high priestess of the club. The place was dark, smoky, and smelled of alcohol, but one could meet friends and make easy acquaintances. I wore a lot of black turtleneck sweaters and my dark hair was long and loose on my back, as was the fashion of those days.

On Rue Jacob, I often went to a bar called Manhattan and met some interesting intellectuals. I was interested in people and people were interested in my art. I still visited Montparnasse from time to time, going to la Coupole to eat clams in wine. The place had a Bohemian flavor in those days and had been the haunt of Gertrude Stein and Ernest Hemingway in the '20s. Other favorite places included the Café Select on Boulevard Raspail, Café du Dome, and Café La Rotonde. I remember meeting Cezar, France's most famous sculptor, at the Café Select and in those early days after World War II. I also met with famous painters like Mané-Katz and Bernard Buffet at la Coupole.

After World War II Paris was not joyous, but it was still a beautiful city. I would go up to Montmartre to sketch the people, to earn a few francs, and to walk along the steep Rue Lepic to arrive at Place du Tertre. Winter was bitter cold, and I would come to a warm café and smell delicious food while my stomach was empty. I would work on portraits in charcoal of the patrons of the restaurant, but I was hungry, sad, and lonely.

When a group of young people, three girls and four boys, decided to leave Paris for the South of France, they asked me to join them, and I accepted eagerly. Early one morning we went to Les Halles to find a truck that would go to Nice empty and return to Paris fully loaded with oranges. I don't remember the trip, as I slept most of the way, but upon opening my eyes I saw mimosas, golden yellow, and skies of blue. As I inhaled the balmy, fragrant air, I thought, this is the place I want to live and paint. I was but sixteen years old. After a few days of camping, and sleeping in a tent (where I almost got raped by one of the boys), I soon left the little group to go on my own, with

Often I would go
hungry while
sketching in the
champs Elysée

the few francs that I had saved in Paris. I found a small room, on a crowded lively street. To my dismay, at night, the same street became a working zone for pimps and prostitutes. Nice had many tourists and a lot of American soldiers visiting on "R and R," or leave. As it turned out, I did very well, sketching the many young soldiers with their temporary dates, and soon I was popular in the bars and cafés of the Rue Halevy, near the Promenade des Anglais. I enjoyed the people of the South of France with their colorful accents, their marketplaces with all the bountiful fruits, vegetables, and fragrant flowers; and the rocky beaches in front of the big hotels. I liked the Carnivals in February that lasted three whole days and nights. On the promenade, people often slumbered in chairs, in the early morning after a night of reveling.

I would often take a train to Villefranche, then a small harbor, about twenty kilometers from Nice. The ships of the American fleet would be anchored there for a short time and the bars, cafés, and sidewalks, would be filled with sailors, eager to enjoy a holiday and get friendly with the local girls. I would sketch these sailors, all neat and clean in their white uniforms. They tipped generously and were so courteous. My English skills improved steadily with practice, in those days in the South of France. I smiled and talked a lot and did some good sketches. For the first time I had plenty of food and I was making a living. I bought myself a print dress and went dancing at the Casino on the Promenade des Anglais in Nice. While riding the train to Villefranche, I went also to Monaco, and admired the beautiful coastline with its rocky mountains, sandy coves, the ultramarine and green waters below. Every place I saw I wanted to paint and vowed to do so, someday.

One day, I learned that a large fleet of American ships was coming to Cannes and I decided to go there for the first time. It took about an hour by bus. In 1947, Cannes was a lovely resort, with its beautiful bay, sandy beaches, and lovely sparkling hotels set on the gleaming harbor. The Carlton, the Majestic, the Martinez hotels and a few smaller ones clung to the surrounding hills. In wintertime many retired elderly people came for the balmy weather; while Parisians, as well as the young people, would come mostly in the summer time. From the first impression, I knew I had to move to Cannes, to live here, to paint here. I found an inexpensive pension not too far from the beach and began working at my portrait sketches in hotel terraces, waterfront cafés, the beach and bars, going from one place to the other. I did rather well when the ships were in port with the sailors ashore. I took some time to go swimming in the Mediterranean and soon acquired a golden tan. I lost my chubbiness and men found me attractive and often propositioned me. But I concentrated on my work and only when I was satisfied that my goal was achieved, that I had completed a certain amount of sketches, would I go dancing or accept an invitation to dine with some handsome officer of the American navy. In Cannes, many beautiful French girls could be seen in the company of officers in civilian clothes. But to be seen with a uniformed sailor might give a girl a bad reputation, and in those days, I cared very much about my image.

I was a romantic, and as I loved the cinema, I was fortunate to be in Cannes when the first international film festival was held at the Majestic Hotel in 1947. I saw my first movie stars including Brigitte Bardot, France's premiere starlet of the cinema. I was excited to be mingling with the glamourous crowds on the terrace of the Majestic Hotel. Starlets everywhere preened for the hordes of photographers. The festival lasted two weeks and thus began a tradition that would put Cannes on the map of the world.

I remember a particularly handsome young lieutenant in the navy who asked me to have dinner with him. His name was Chad and he was from the suburbs of Chicago. I had never seen a more handsome young man. He had a perfect nose, lips, eyes, golden blond hair, and he was so romantic. We chose a restaurant in St Paul de Vence, an old hillside village of Provence. It was my first time to visit the interior of Provence. After the taxi climbed the hill, we stepped out in front of a lovely old inn and restaurant overlooking the hills and valley. The dinner was wonderful, the candlelight soft, the fireplace glowing in the room, and the bed large with its thick down cover. I remember soft music on the radio, Chad's tender caresses and lovemaking, our last poignant hug when he left and our many kisses. I was happy, sad, in a dream world. Early morning at dawn, he was gone and I heard a cock crow in the distant hills. It was my first romantic experience.

The countryside of Provence had awakened in me a desire to paint, to put colors on canvas. I thought that taking a trip to a foreign country would inspire me even more. Summer was over, and in the early fall, my girlfriend Colette and I took a train to Italy. Our destination was Capri. First we stopped in Rome and I remember visiting the museums, the Forum, the carriage ride on the Via Veneto. All the while young Italian men whistled at us, at Colette with her blonde hair and blue eyes, and me, very tan with dark hair.

It was when we arrived in Naples that Colette and I parted, as I had met Lt. Brent Fletcher, a young American navy officer, stationed in Naples. He had a lovely apartment on Via Posilippo. We became lovers and were together for a month. One day I went to Capri, took a small boat, and at a beautiful site, I painted two large canvases in brilliant colors. The subject was the

St Paul de Vence
my first Romantic
affair.

Faraglione, the rocks surrounded by aquamarine water and cerulean skies. As money ran short, I took shelter with fishermen and their families and shared their meals of spaghetti and Chianti wine, for a few sketches in payment.

When I returned to Cannes, I found out I was pregnant. It was distressing to me and the people at the pension were very concerned and advised me to return to Naples to see what my friend could do. Brent had been a decent young man, but it was only an infatuation. However, I decided to return to Naples and went to Brent. He was understandably concerned and took me to a woman who performed an abortion. The blood and the cramps: it was grueling! Brent left me in a comfortable hotel room near the waterfront and saw me every day, until I was able to leave Naples.

Upon returning to Cannes, I resumed my life, with my work, sketching portraits. My two paintings of the Faraglione of Capri, were exhibited at the restaurant where I was sketching people dining, "Symphonie chez Freddy," at Palm Beach, an exclusive section of Cannes. The restaurant had an elegant garden filled with flowers on small tables, soft light, and music. Freddy was the genial host and a patron of the arts. One evening, a handsome, smartly dressed young man invited me to have a glass of champagne at his table. I politely declined, as I knew the rules, but Freddy, who was there, told me to accept the invitation as he knew the young man and the elegant party at his table. His name was Jasper Markham and he belonged to a prominent and wealthy family from New York. The group was well bred and sophisticated. I had acquired enough English to sustain the conversation and all seemed to find me charming. Jasper and I became lovers the next night. I was very taken by his savoir-faire, his charm, and his polished manners. At the Palm Beach Casino we dined and then danced until dawn on the outdoor dance floor to mambo and cha-cha rhythms. I was a good dancer and Jasper was proud to show me off to his friends, young cosmopolitans and a few titled Englishmen. I fantasized sometimes how life would be to be married to him but the season was over and we each went our own way. Twenty years later I saw Jasper in New York and over an intimate dinner at the Pierre Hotel, we reminisced. He told me that I was more desirable than ever. However, we were both married at the time and my infatuation with him was long gone.

I often thought of my brother Dédé in New York, and received news of him from time to time. He was well, going to school and adjusting to his new life, parents, and friends. They lived in a suburb called Forest Hills. I thought often of the day that I would most certainly go there. When I would be ready for America, my dream. . . .

I was now living in Cannes in a small one-room furnished apartment, close to the beach, in a rather pleasant modern building. I kept working at my portraits, going back and forth from Cannes to Nice, and often to Juan les Pins. Juan les Pins was very much in vogue in those days, with patrons staying up late, dancing at the Club Maxim's or listening to the jazz of Sydney Bechet at La Pinede, and finishing in the wee hours at Pam Pam. We would often return to Cannes in a convertible with the top down, six or seven young people, watching the sun rise on the blue dawn of the Mediterranean, exhilarated by the music and life. On one of my trips to Nice, while sketching in a bar, I met a young American soldier. He was on leave from occupied Germany. His name was Scott and he was of Nordic extraction. He was very fair, slight of build, and had gentle blue eyes and sensual lips. His family lived in California. We talked much of the time about America. He was polite and never propositioned me. Most of the time he was alone and didn't associate with any of the groups of soldiers crowding the bars. Scott and I took long walks on the beach and he would tell me of his plans when he returned home. When his two-week vacation was over, just before he was to go back to his duty in occupied Germany, we spent the night together. He was shy and very gentle. It was pleasant and we promised to write to each other. Previously I had experienced more pain than pleasure in the sexual act but with Scott it was different. I relaxed more, and I thought that all was well.

The Riviera setting was so romantic, the casinos glittering, the bay with the lights sparkling as jewels in a necklace, the restaurants joyful, music always present. Except for the Art Academie, the museums, and St. Germain, I really didn't miss Paris, and it was with a renewed pleasure that I contemplated my return to Cannes on the few trips I took. After being on the Riviera several months I did visit Paris via train. From the train window I would grab a bunch of fragrant golden mimosa and bring it to my face to smell its sweet scent. Many years later I would live in a villa near Grasse where perfumes were made from the gathered essence of flowers grown in the hills and valleys of Provence.

I received letters from Scott, from Germany, telling me he missed me with sweet endearing words. I replied to him that I thought of him a lot and always sent a photo of myself. He was twenty years old; I was a little younger.

Cannes in the summertime had many tourists from New York and from European cities. The Carlton terrace was crowded every evening at cocktail time. We young girls would dress our best and sit at a table and sometimes the prettiest of us got invited to dinner and perhaps a nightclub and casino. I was a curious extrovert. I was fortunate to be asked to dine many evenings by men of various ages, and was pleased to be seated at fancy restaurants among the well-dressed crowd. After dinner I would often refuse to accompany my dates to their hotels, usually with the excuse that I had to work at my sketches the next morning. While I was curious about sexuality, I was not promiscuous, just selective.

Cannes had always been a haven for homosexuals and in the early fifties, one could see beautiful boys descend in pairs, from Paris, New York, and Rome. They had their own special beaches and bars. One evening as I was sitting in the Trois Cloches, a bar that catered to gay men, I had done some portraits, and had my sketchpad on my lap. I noticed two very handsome young Scandinavian boys looking at me. They invited me for a drink and after sketching their portraits, for which they promptly tipped me generously, they ordered another round of drinks. I was feeling giddy and lightheaded, just enjoying their company. Soon we left the place, singing, hand in hand. I found myself in a hotel room in bed with these two young men. The most exciting thing was that we all slept naked, and caressed each other, but without any sexual contact. Their bodies were beautiful, tanned and muscular, not unlike Michaelangelo's models. It was a nurturing and esthetic experience for me.

I had girlfriends in whom I would confide. Often, at the Café Terrasse, we would sit facing the waterfront and, over a drink, talk of our men, romance, even sex, as in France, we were open and casual about it. One of my girlfriends, a striking, very tall brunette with a statuesque body, would seek me out. Her manner was a little mannish. She had olive skin and large brown eyes and sensual lips. Her name was Odile. One day she came to my apartment and we started to discuss men and sex. On the subject of climax, I was a little naive and told her I never experienced that sensation and was curious. The feeling she described was unknown to me, so she promptly endeavored to teach me. We lay side by side on my bed and she showed me exactly what to do to myself, which exact spot. After a while as I lay there and nothing happened, she told me to be patient and to persevere. I did and suddenly, quick as a flash, I climaxed and it was like a thousand volts. Afterward, I felt a little ashamed, but nevertheless had achieved another experience.

It was a gorgeous summer in 1952. The beaches were crowded, the hotels full, and I was working at my sketches. I was making good money, so I bought clothes and jewelry. I had a slender, shapely figure with a tiny waistline. Often as I walked by the terraces and cafés, men would whistle at me even though I was clutching my sketchbook against my full, round bosom. I wore a lot of low-cut dresses and high heels. It was hot in the evenings and the nights were romantic. You could see on the Croisette couples hand in hand, mostly American sailors with beautiful French girls. The young dashing officers, clean-shaven, smelling of cologne and dressed in civilian clothes, always could be recognized by their shiny black regulation shoes. The local young men were good looking, but short, and often had the smell of garlic on their breath. They also were a little envious of the American sailors, as many local girls would favor them.

Scott would write often now, and his letters became pressing and serious. He was talking marriage, that he loved me. There is a custom in France, if a young girl is not married by the time she turns twenty-five, she would have to wear a Sainte Catherine hat and become an old maid. I didn't relish that idea, so marrying Scott was one solution to that problem. But seriously, I felt I had not experienced enough of life, and before settling down, I wanted to live fully, excitedly, so I wrote Scott that I cared for him and was looking forward to his visit, but not committing myself at that time.

In the meanwhile, I was going out a lot, dating and dancing at Palm Beach, after my work was done, often finishing the evening at Whisky a Go Go until four or five in the morning. Breakfast would be café and croissant at the Petit Carlton café, Rue d' Antibes. Sitting at the bar, drinking anisette and pernod, were off duty hotel clerks, late casino gamblers, and prostitutes with runs in their stockings. One early evening, upon terminating my day of sketching portraits, the skies were golden with a flamboyant sunset, the sea calm and iridescent, reflecting the blue ridges of the Esterel Mountains. I was walking along the Croisette, clad only in a blue top and short shorts, with my slender legs showing their tan and my firm breasts jiggling. I noticed a car following me. It was not unusual, as the Croisette was a favorite strip to pick up girls. Many prostitutes worked there. I always ignored the cars and the men in them and they understood and left me alone. What was different with this car is that it was persistent and as I glanced over my shoulder, I saw a couple in the car. They kept on following me. After a while, I thought they must be tourists, possibly foreign, and might need some information, so I slowed down my pace. The car stopped and in broken French, the man at the wheel asked me some questions. He was grinning and looking at me. I quickly responded in English as they were obviously American. They were relieved that I spoke their language and we conversed for a few minutes. They were from New York and had enjoyed their first visit to Cannes. Would I get in the car, they asked, as the other motorists were becoming impatient. I got in the car and we chatted for some time, comparing food, French customs, and local flowers. They were in their forties and married. At the end of the Croisette, where the road stops and goes uphill, they asked if they could invite me for a drink. I had no particular rendezvous, so I acquiesced. As we drove on, I was happy to practice my English and told my new friends of my desire to go to New York as I had a brother living there and my dream was to join him. It was getting dark but we soon arrived in a graveled courtyard in the entrance of a small hotel. We passed the concierge and arrived in a room with no furniture except a large bed. From the adjacent bathroom the man produced a bottle of bourbon and poured us each a full glass. After awhile, I felt dizzy, not having had dinner. It was getting darker and we were all sitting at the edge of the bed making small talk. The man put his arms around me and started to stroke me and kiss me. He gently pushed me down on the bed and proceeded to undress me, to remove my top and shorts. Soon they were both making love to me and things were as if in slow motion. I was lying there, with my head light from the alcohol and sensations I had never before experienced. It was pleasurable but it was an unsettling experience and one I didn't care to repeat. However, things were to be different when I arrived in New York years later.

One day, Odile came to see me, to tell me that she met a handsome man, an American, and that she would like for me to say hello to him. We had a rendezvous at the Carlton Beach the next morning. We would often parade there in our smallest bikinis. My bikini was white to set off my tan. I soon saw Odile and waved to her. She looked spectacular in a crimson bikini and a large straw sun hat. We chatted awhile and after an hour, I left.

As I was walking on the sand, on the water's edge, I saw the beautiful body of a man with short cropped sandy hair, but what arrested me was his face, with the most luminous green eyes matching the color of the sea. He looked like a Greek god. I stood in awe as he approached me and said that I must be Odile's friend. As I nodded, he extended his hand to me. We introduced ourselves. He was very tall and as we walked the beach he had to stoop to talk to me. His name was Lance Garrett. Soon we were sitting at a table in the shade of a café, enjoying a drink. I told him of my work and ambitions. He seemed genuinely interested in my description of my paintings and my ambitions to go to America. I spotted Odile from a distance but, if she saw us, she didn't care to disturb us as we were very intent and in a world of our own. Lance was a lieutenant in the American navy; his ship was part of the fleet in the Bay of Cannes. I was mesmerized and totally under his charm. It was difficult contemplating to leave him that afternoon, but he had ship duty.

The next day was Bastille Day, the fourteenth of July. It was the height of the holiday season. Everyone was looking forward to the festivities, dancing at the Casino, with fireworks illuminating the town and harbor. Young men and women put on their best attires for this glorious French celebration. I was sad to have left Lance, but overjoyed when soon he asked me to dinner and dancing at the Palm Beach Casino for the next day. I could hardly contain myself and counted the hours. When he rang my doorbell, he was wearing a light seersucker suit, with a white shirt and blue tie, but I only saw his eyes, green with a sparkle, looking tenderly at me. His voice was deep and he spoke slowly to compliment me on my looks. I was wearing a low cut dress of white satin, to set off my tan and my dark, shiny hair. We were a striking couple, strolling the Croisette. We stopped for cocktails at the terrace of the Hotel Martinez and dined by soft candlelight. The food was delicious, the wine excellent. We were holding hands and gazing at each other with desire. I was so enthralled and aglow, when we arrived at the Palm Beach to view the fireworks and to dance. The lovely terrace facing the sea was crowded with well-dressed people. Soon the fireworks started in the indigo skies. It was a scintillation of a thousand colored sparks exploding all at once. It was magic, much enhanced by the presence of Lance. We danced, close together, and found ourselves back in my apartment. After much kissing and fierce, passionate, tender lovemaking, in the early dawn, Lance left. I found myself hugging my pillow that smelled of his after shave cologne. I had never met a man, who spoke so many words of endearment.

I was sure it was love, a desperate situation. Here I was, practically engaged to one man, and with all the passion of my heart I wanted another. The next day was a sad one as Lance told me that his ship was the first to leave early in the morning to do some maneuvers in the Mediterranean off the coast of Spain. Barcelona was the port in which they would anchor with the rest of the fleet to follow later. We were both sad to leave one another, not knowing when in the distant future we would see each other again. Life was not fair. Lance had awakened a passion and love in me that I did not know I possessed. My body ached for his. That night, as I cried in his arms, I knew that I had made up my mind to follow him to Barcelona, to see him one more time. I had embarked on a passionate romance and longed for a human being as I never had before. My thought of Scott, who was shortly to come to Cannes, was far from my mind at that moment.

I had only received one short letter from Lance since his departure from

Cannes. He assured me of his love and that his ship was to be in port for three days in Barcelona. We were to meet at the Excelsior Hotel. Early one morning, I took the train from Cannes to Barcelona. It was a long and tiring journey. After we passed the border and entered Spain, I felt elated and forgot how tired I was. The train stopped at the ancient Barcelona station and I took a taxi to the hotel where Lance had reserved a room for us. I took a long hot bath, changed clothes, and walked out to the Ramblas dei Flores, one of the main promenades of Barcelona. The looks of the people, the language, all was different from France. I enjoyed the exotic atmosphere. In anticipation of seeing Lance, my heart pounded fast. I was in a state of great exaltation and excitement.

Around eight o'clock, in the cocktail lounge of the hotel, I saw him. He was wearing his civilian clothes, smiling, with a tender look in his beautiful green eyes. I was trembling with emotion as he gently kissed my cheeks, as in French greeting. Soon after drinks and dinner, we were walking hand in hand along the narrow streets of old Barcelona. At night, it was enchanting, seeing the illuminated fountains, the streets full of people. In the flamenco dancing hall where we stopped, I was enthralled to hear the rhythmic new sounds, the tapping of feet and clicking of castanets, and to see the dancing by the slim-waisted young Spanish men and women, clad in colorful costumes. I was experiencing the magic of romance, being with Lance. That night after passionate lovemaking, Lance cradled me in his arms and after a while we slept. We had two more wonderful days in Barcelona, exploring the city, loving each other, but there was a dark cloud on the horizon. The ship was sailing, this time for the port of Valencia. We agreed that I was to go there by train, and wait for Lance, who was to ask for a leave of absence for two days. The time passed quickly after he left, and I took a train for Valencia. Soon, he would be gone back to America, to his home in Vermont. I ached at the thought of it.

Valencia was a pleasant city. I remember the orange trees, the pastel houses and buildings, an air of fiesta and gaiety. Here it was balmy and light, the sky very blue. Lance arrived at the small but quaint hotel, its walls covered with bougainvilleas. For the first time in a long time I had a longing to paint, to record the scene, my sad happiness, my love.

We spent lots of time making love, our bodies glistening with perspiration, in the lovely room overlooking a small plaza filled with flowers. I counted the hours, while sitting on a chair and watching Lance slowly dress. The ship was to sail at dawn and I was to accompany him to the docks before he departed for Lisbon and America. At four o'clock in the morning, we took a taxicab for the Port of Valencia. As we approached, we saw sailors swarming around the docks, with sleepy Spanish girls clinging to them until their last goodbyes.

Sad tears rolled down my cheeks. After a last kiss, Lance boarded the tender that was to take him to his ship. I stood there for the longest time holding my wet handkerchief, until he finally disappeared. Then slowly I returned to our hotel, to make my preparation to leave. We had agreed to write to each other and to see one another in America, where I was sure to go. Lance was an only son and talked fondly of his widowed mother. I had confided to him of my life and the tragedy of my childhood. So, in the short time that we spent together, we had tried to get the most of our different backgrounds into perspective.

The prospect of returning to Cannes was unappealing. This was my first visit to Spain. I took the train to Madrid to see the paintings of Goya at the Prado Museum, and also visited Toledo and Escurial. I arrived in Madrid on a glorious morning. After settling in a small pension, I started to explore the city. My first encounter was Plaza Mayor, where pigeons gathered in flocks, then on to the popular districts, the Bodegas, the Prado museum, with its magnificent Goyas, the palaces, churches and cathedrals. I experienced all with enthusiasm. I walked the city endlessly. I went to my first bullfight at Plaza de Toros, where I enjoyed the pageantry. With a sketchbook that I had purchased, I made many quick sketches of the Corrida. I took in everything: the crowd, the toros, the matadors, the picadors, the musicians. It was all new and very exciting. Later I wandered in smoky Bodegas, where animated groups of men were talking about the Corrida and the kills and the bravest matador who received two ears and the tail of the bull.

Dusk had settled in the city and I was still walking. I arrived at the Hilton Hotel and sat on a stool in the cool bar. It had been a hot afternoon and I had walked several miles. Not far from me, a couple of seats away, sat a young man of rather stocky build with bushy brown hair and a pleasant face. He looked at me and smiled. After a few halting words in bad Spanish, he asked if he could sit next to me. I answered in French, that, yes, he could. Over a drink, I discovered that he was an American on vacation in Spain to practice his Spanish. I told him I was an art student on my first visit to Madrid. He had been in the city for some time, and he offered to show me the sights. Since he was friendly and clean looking, I accepted. His name was Skip. He had a robust laugh and a fun-loving nature. During the following two days, as we strolled by shops, arcades, cafés, I was drawn to him due to his exceedingly optimistic nature. Skip liked his drinks, particularly Scotch, but he never got drunk, just pleasantly high and cheerful. All in all, Skip was a good companion in Madrid.

One evening as we were walking toward the pension where I lived, I felt sad and lonely, thinking of Lance and longing for him. Skip was getting amorous and his affectionate hugs and squeezes were soothing to me, but only to a certain point would I allow him to get romantic. We had arrived near the pension when Skip had an idea. Why don't we stay together the rest of the night and enjoy each other's company? We were both tired so we started to walk to find a place to have a drink and talk. In those days, Spain was a very puritanical country. A single girl, unmarried, could not bring a man to her room at the pension, so we continued our walk in search of a hotel. We kept on walking the streets in the warm night of Madrid.

The middle of the night found us near a narrow alley, where a sign said "Hotel." We rang the bell. A woman came to the door and, after we had asked for a room, she ushered us up the stairs. The place was plush, the room done in garnet with rococo lamps, complete with bidet in the private bathroom. Skip paid the woman. Once alone, we realized that we were in a Spanish bordello. It was hilarious to us and, exhausted, we both fell asleep. Twenty years later, I saw Skip in San Francisco where we were then both living. Over a lovely dinner we reminisced and laughed about that episode in Madrid.

Upon my return to Cannes, I found letters from Scott waiting for me. The last one announced that he had taken two weeks leave from Germany and would arrive in Cannes shortly. Hastily I answered back that all was well and I was looking forward to his return.

Chapter Two

I N THE EARLY FIFTIES, while living in Cannes, I met some interesting people who later had the opportunity to help me in my life. I remember the
time I was enjoying myself in the pool at the Cap d'Antibes Eden Roc,
my tanned figure showing in my tiny bikini. Of the young men sunbathing
and swimming, who were courting me, a short, rotund, and jovial fellow was
a constant suitor. He was an Egyptian named Osmanli Fariba, very well
known in Hollywood circles and knew many of the celebrities staying at
Hotel du Cap. Casually at the bar he introduced me to Hunt Albanese, a tall
gray-haired gentleman who had a hotel and casino in Las Vegas, Nevada. I
told Hunt that I desired very much to go to America, but would need a job and
a sponsor. He replied, "We always need pretty, young, talented French girls,"
and wrote down my name and address. Later I was to receive a formal contract to work at his casino as a showgirl and artist. Years later I took advan-
tage of his offer when I had to establish residence in Las Vegas for my first
divorce. I worked at the El Rancho Vegas Hotel as an artist for a few months.
There I met many celebrities while I was sketching their portraits.

A man who also influenced my life, later, when I came to America, was
Bud Anson. We had met in the cocktail lounge of the Hotel Carlton in Cannes.
He and his wife were among a small group of people from Dallas, Texas, who
were touring Europe. We struck up a friendship. While Bud's wife and the
other members of the tour were busy shopping and sightseeing, he and I
would sit on the terrace, enjoying cold drinks. I did many sketches of him. He
was in his early fifties, a stocky man with short cropped gray hair and a thick
Texas accent. I found him generous and cordial. I saw somewhat of a father
image in him. When he proposed to invite me to go to Paris for the coming
weekend as the tour was departing, I accepted, and Bud promptly bought me
a round-trip train ticket. It was an opportunity to see Paris again in style.

Bud had booked a room for me in the same hotel where the tour was staying, the Intercontinental, only two floors below Bud's and his wife's room. He called me as soon as I arrived, as the tour group had taken a plane earlier. We went shopping. Bud bought me a lovely camel coat, a suit, and some lingerie. We lunched at Maxim's and I felt very special.

Bud needed feminine companionship as he explained that his wife was busy with charity work. She was also disinterested in sex and was alcoholic. I was a good listener and he didn't force himself upon me. To my great fear of being caught, he visited my room while his wife was asleep. He would make love to me for a brief moment as he ejaculated quickly. It was intriguing but also dangerous. I thought the situation amusing. Bud said upon leaving that if I ever came to America, he would help me. He owned a chain of hardware stores all over Texas and lived on a big ranch. I jotted his business telephone number in my little black book with the other names for possible future use. I realized that this was calculating, but I was, after all, a survivor.

I returned to Cannes, to my work and my friends. Scott arrived in the early spring of '53. Scott wore his khaki uniform and, under his visored cap, his eyes matched the color of the skies. We spent some lovely days sunbathing and swimming at the beach, and lunching at sidewalk cafés. We got married on a beautiful sunny day in the City Hall of Cannes in the company of only our two witnesses. Then we proceeded to a formal photo session that took place at Le Suquet. I was wearing a white lace suit and a small hat with a veil. Scott looked solemn in a dark suit and tie.

In lieu of a honeymoon we spent two days in Monaco. I remember sitting on a bench in the lovely garden by the Casino of Monte Carlo, with Scott at my side, taking photos. I wondered, "What is in store for me?"

Scott had asked for a transfer from Germany to France for the remaining six months of his service in Europe. We were to go to the army base stationed at the port of La Rochelle on the Brittany coast. As I made the last preparation to leave Cannes, I felt sad, saying goodbye to all my friends. But, I was now married. I was Mrs. Scott Chauncey and I was soon to go to America.

La Rochelle was a dull place, an old city and port. Scott was working at the army base and I was idle most of the time. I wrote to Lance. In his last letter, he had given me his address in Vermont. In La Rochelle time passed quickly, and soon, Scott received orders that he was being transferred to an army base in Anchorage, Alaska for his last year of duty. But before departure he was allowed a month's leave. We spent a few days in Paris, which was nostalgic for me. It was to be ten long years before I returned to the City of Lights. We took the Bateau-Mouche on the Seine River, went to the top of the

Eiffel Tower, and walked the Champs Elysées. I obtained my visa from the American Embassy as the wife of a military man. After a last long look at the Paris skyline from our hotel room, we took the flight for New York. From there we stopped in Los Angeles on our way to Alaska.

I could not contain my happiness at the prospect of seeing my brother Dédé again, to witness how he had changed and to see his new surroundings. When we arrived at the New York airport, we took a taxi to Forest Hills, where Mama Vanya, his adoptive mother, and Dédé lived. His adoptive father had died. My brother had become a tall, husky youth, with dark blond hair, blue eyes, and fair skin. It was a very emotional reunion. Mama Vanya gave Scott and me her bedroom, and we got settled in the small apartment. Andy, as my brother was called now, was going to high school and working part-time. Mama Vanya was a tiny lady with twinkling eyes, who was much devoted to Andy.

The next evening found Andy, Scott and me admiring the lights of Broadway at night. It was a fantastic feeling, walking between my brother and my husband in New York City, U.S.A. I took in everything: the pulsating rhythm of the city, the people, the sounds. We went to the Empire State Building, saw the Rockettes at Radio City Music Hall, Rockerfeller Plaza, Central Park, and returned home tired but elated. It was time to leave after a few days of visiting.

Giving my dear brother Andy a last embrace, Scott and I took another plane across the American land to Los Angeles. Scott's mother lived in a small, white-shingled house in a nondescript area. She was an angular woman, vaguely Nordic looking, who greeted us warmly. But I had some difficulty in understanding her. She was separated from her husband, who lived in another suburb. We met Scott's father later for dinner in a restaurant overlooking the ocean at Santa Monica. He was a slight man with a warm personality. He worked as an aviation consultant. After this short visit, we took a plane to Seattle and on to Anchorage, Alaska, our final destination.

It was now fall, yet seemed the middle of winter to me. Anchorage in those days of 1953 was still a frontier town. There was a main drag, a couple of parallel streets, a few stores, a gift shop, bars, restaurant, the Westward Hotel, and a television station. The military base was many miles away where the army provided housing for soldiers and their dependents. We had a base apartment consisting of two rooms, kitchen and bath, in a large building housing several of the soldiers' families. It was extremely cold and snowed days on end. That winter I had to get up at four thirty in the morning to cook Scott's breakfast of bacon and eggs. It was always the same. He had to leave by six to be at the base to report for work. I would return to bed. I was bored. To occupy my time, I decided to write a short story of my romance with Lance. I found a typewriter and with two fingers, typed ten or fifteen pages. I soon grew tired of it. I accepted doing some photo modeling for advertising. I got tired of that, also.

I wrote to Lance and secured a post office box for my mail so Scott wouldn't know about my correspondence. I was wondering what Lance was doing now that he was out of the navy and at home. Winter evenings were long, we didn't have any friends and Scott was getting irritable. I took pleasure in taking an early bus and going to downtown Anchorage to Main Street to the only gift and souvenir shop. The friendly couple who managed it had accepted me as a regular visitor as I perused the Eskimo carvings, Alaskan fur hats, boots, and other souvenirs that G.I.s would buy and send home. One day in the shop I was introduced to the producer of the local television program for children. Soon I found myself with the job of a majorette for the kiddies' show, in costume and twirling a baton. To find a majorette costume in Alaska was difficult. It had to be of white satin and a tall hat with pompoms. No such costume was to be had in all Anchorage, so I hired a seamstress to make one for me. My work was pleasant at the station and I was earning some good money that I would promptly send to Lance in the form of money orders so he could put it in the bank for me. I wondered when I would be able to visit him.

Scott grew more irritable each day, smoking cigarette after cigarette and drinking more when he got home from the base. Our contacts were few, the lovemaking strained and unsatisfactory. Scott was not worldly enough for me and I was sad. I didn't like the building we lived in, so noisy and little privacy with its many women and children. The only bus to Anchorage left early in the morning. Life on the base was depressing. Scott and I had arguments. We finally decided to move to downtown Anchorage. We found an authentic log cabin and moved in. The place was simple, a large room with the necessary furniture and household goods for housekeeping. It was primitive but within walking distance to Main Street and the television station.

We had a quiet period then. I kept on working as winter progressed. Despite the same gray, cold, depressing days, the Eskimo race went on. In the short time I worked at the TV station I grew restless and worried with Scott's meager pay. Now that we didn't live on base, life was more expensive in town. I had not realized that we would have these problems. As we had to pay dearly for milk, eggs, and meat, we barely made ends meet. Scott was nervous, irritable, a glazed look often in his eyes. I always wondered why we didn't have any friends. Something was wrong, but I could not find out what. We seldom made love anymore. We did not communicate much, and I was becoming a bit frightened of him. When he would drink, he would often become abusive. I confided to the lady in the gift shop and she said that with behavior like this, it could only get worse. She advised me to take precautions and the sooner I left him, the better it would be for me.

I had been in Anchorage for ten months yet it seemed years to me. After careful planning, I decided to leave Scott, for some time to myself. I purchased a one-way ticket to Seattle and San Francisco. I left the log cabin early one morning, after leaving a note for Scott, saying I wanted a separation. I learned later upon discovery of the note that Scott was so enraged that he came to the airport with a loaded rifle after me. But I was on my way to my destiny, bound for San Francisco.

On board the plane, I made friends with a nice young stewardess to whom I told my story. She was very sympathetic of my plight and offered me hospitality in the apartment that she shared with two other airline stewardesses. To reassure me, she gave me the name of her brother-in-law, a divorce attorney. I accepted all in gratitude and thought it was a good omen. After a few days of looking for a place in San Francisco, I found a nice residential hotel on Sutter Street, near Union Square, and moved in. I was enchanted with this city, its glorious bay, the hills, Chinatown, North Beach, Fisherman's Wharf, Nob Hill, and nearby Sausalito. I explored the various exotic places, but on my more serious moments I thought of work, of getting a job. I had written to the attorney and I knew I would need money for my divorce and to live. I also wrote to Lance that I was in San Francisco and that my thoughts were always with him. As I walked the busy streets of San Francisco, I chanced upon an open place, more a garage than a gallery, but full of paintings. A nice middle-aged man welcomed me. As we talked, I told him that I was an artist, looking for a job, that I was French and had done portrait work. This European man asked me to join him that evening. He would introduce me to one of his friends, a man, who owned a very well known restaurant and night club called Bimbo's 365. I thanked him and that evening, with my sketchbook under my arm, I went to the club. My benevolent friend was there, and soon introduced me to the owner, Mister Guido Belmonte, a kind, old-fashioned Italian man. I sketched my new friend, who had a picturesque face with bushy eyebrows. I could start to work right away. Of course I had to pay a percentage of my tips to the owner. But I was elated and felt confident in my abilities.

Bimbo's, situated on Columbus Avenue, occupied almost a whole block. In 1953, it was a plush night club. Through glass doors the patrons entered a foyer. To the right was a hat check room and to the left a large cocktail lounge with a piano bar. Along the far wall, a long bar had a dozen stools and small tables with attractive red lamps on them. In the middle of the cocktail lounge, a curious glass contraption, more of a modern wooden sculpture, had an aquarium inside with a tiny nude figure of a girl in the fish bowl. Down a few stairs from the cocktail lounge, was the large dining room, more the size of a ballroom. Tables were set with small lamps and flowers, and at the very end, a beautiful stage, with dark red velvet curtains, with an orchestra in the background. It was the best night club outside of Las Vegas!

I remember going to work at six o'clock in the evenings until 2 A.M. I had leisurely days, the weather was perfect, the sky very blue. I loved San Francisco. I had purchased a sketch pad, crayon conté, charcoals, a costume of a black satin blouse with a large bow, black fishnet stockings, a small red beret on my short dark hair and high heeled shoes. My blouse was low cut to reveal my cleavage. As I finished the portraits and men were watching me, I would put my tips in my brassiere. The atmosphere of the lounge was lively and I enjoyed working to the tinkling of the piano, mixed with the sounds of the sing-a-longs. The old ragtime songs and music amused the patrons while they drank and partied before dinner and the floor show.

The men tipped generously to get portraits of wives or girl friends. I had to work fast, in semi-darkness. I used gray charcoal paper, charcoal, and white conté crayons for highlights. The sketches were flattering resemblances and people liked my work. I was getting good practice. Two months passed and I heard from the attorney that in California, I had to wait a year to get a divorce. Or I could take another step and go to the state of Nevada, establish a residency for five weeks and get an uncontested divorce. The attorney was in contact with Scott and had notified him of my intentions. I was not in a hurry to get the divorce, as being married afforded me a certain protection in my new country. What I had in mind was to return to New York to see my brother and to see Lance. But San Francisco was so beautiful, so friendly, that I kept postponing my trip.

The club had some excellent first-class revues, big-time singers, the Blue Bell chorus girls, comedians, and ventriloquists. I enjoyed watching it all from behind the curtain. One evening, the French ventriloquist, who was the star of the show, needed an assistant for his act. This act had a duck puppet with a long neck and a yellow beak. The ventriloquist would do a "Barber of

Portrait
Sketching at various
clubs in San Francisco

Seville" hilarious comedic parody with the duck. Jacques Martin was elated when I accepted his offer to be his assistant. I had to wear a tight showgirl costume that showed a lot of bosom. Then I had to stand still, facing the audience while Jacques would do his routine. I had a bit of stage fright but as soon as the audience started to applaud, I felt more at ease. The act lasted twelve to fifteen minutes. The experience was exhilarating, especially when people laughed and applauded as the duck puppet ogled appreciatively at my ample cleavage.

In between my sketching were two nightly shows. The act lasted two weeks. Jacques Martin had coached me well. What I enjoyed most at that time was to share the dressing room with the show girls of the revue, to see them apply their make up, false eye lashes and their glittering costumes. The show business atmosphere, their comments about men and their love affairs was all fun and new to me.

One evening an attractive, well-dressed young man invited me to have a drink. I was allowed to drink with the customers as it was good for business. He was wearing a gray suit and had reddish wavy hair. I noticed a small diamond ring on his pinkie. I thought he must be wealthy. We talked at great length. I sketched his portrait. He had a roguish way about him that I liked. I was invited often for a drink by businessmen, visiting salesmen, or sailors from the Alameda base. Many times I was told that lonesome men were happy just to talk to a pretty young artist. Miles Sherwyn, that was his name, intrigued me. He asked me to have a late supper. We went to Vanessi's, which was one of my very favorite places, on Broadway. During the evening, Miles confided that he was married to a Romanian woman and at the present time was separated. I told him of my situation with Scott. Miles was the only son of a well-respected dentist. I found him charming, a little egocentric, but sophisticated. We had more dates. I was curious to see where he lived. One evening I asked Miles to show me his house. As his wife was away, we drove to the top of Twin Peaks to a cul-de-sac with a modest two-bedroom house. In the early Fifties there were houses that were identical in architecture and pastel colors. After showing me inside, we proceeded to the bedroom where we made love. I resisted a little. It certainly seemed a little perverted of Miles to make love in his matrimonial bed, but after a while it added spice to our affair. I had saved a little money, and I was preparing myself to leave for New York. I had been in San Francisco four months and I vowed to return to this beautiful city one day.

I arrived in New York, after a visit with Andy, who was now eighteen years old and had enlisted in the navy. I got a room at the Gotham Hotel in Manhattan. I was happy to be near my brother. He had some free time before being assigned to a base. My priorities, after I had called Lance, were to spend some time with my brother and to find a job. I needed money to live on and also to help Andy with what I could. Next to the Gotham Hotel was an Italian Restaurant called El Borracho. Patrons would descend a few stairs to find a typical Italian trattoria, complete with a long bar and a large dining room with candles in holders of Chianti bottles, set upon red-checkered tablecloths. I charmed the owners into letting me work in the evenings, sketching portraits of the patrons. I would arrive in my little costume and beret with my French accent and my sketch pad. I was an instant hit. It worked well, and I started to know the clients. One evening sitting at the bar was a good looking couple: the blond woman, my age, was speaking French. She was wearing a smart black suit and a small veiled hat. The young man looked typical of the clients of the restaurant. He could have been a stockbroker, salesman, office worker, or from the garment district on Seventh Avenue. They offered me a cocktail. He was Ted and she, Lyvia. We became friends and soon Lyvia came often to the restaurant. I had told her my story and she was sympathetic. Sometimes she would invite me to lunch at her smartly decorated apartment on Riverside Drive. She worked as a decorator and had many gentlemen friends, some much older than she. A few of her friends were from out of town. We would go to dinner with her friends who needed feminine company and I enjoyed the luxury of fine cuisine and beautiful restaurants.

Lance and I talked often on the phone but I had not decided to leave New York yet. I wanted to enjoy this place and postponed my meeting with Lance. After a month had passed, I moved out of the Gotham Hotel, to my first apartment in New York, a brownstone a few blocks from Third Avenue, near Fifty-fifth Street. I had a small bedroom, a sitting room, a tiny kitchen and a bathroom. For me, luxury. It was an old building but nicely kept. Across the hall lived a brother and sister. I got very friendly with them, especially with the brother, Jason. He was a handsome young man who worked in a law firm. We became lovers. Jason was college educated and I was impressed with his erudition. He would meet me at P. J. Clarks' on Third Avenue. We would often go to Fire Island on weekends to meet with his college friends. I was acquiring bits and pieces of Americana, including some slang words in my now fluent vocabulary. Jason's sister became quite jealous.

I was doing well at the restaurant so I moved out of the brownstone to a large, well-lit room with windows facing a small courtyard with a tree. It was gaily furnished in white and green naugahyde, a sofa bed, table, chairs, white walls. It gave me the feeling of having my first studio. I bought myself an easel, paints and canvas. I was determined to become a serious artist. I first painted a full length self portrait in front of the large mirror. I was wearing black velvet pants, a white blouse with ruffles at the neckline, and black shoes. I painted the background crimson for contrast. Soon I was using some of my new friends or young men I met at various bars for models.

I left for Vermont to see Lance. He lived in a medium-sized city with lovely rolling hills. Located near the center of town, his home was a modest suburban house, with a garden in the back. It was getting near the Christmas holidays when I arrived. I hadn't seen Lance for more than a year, and he greeted me with passionate kisses. His mother was a lovely lady who greeted me with much affection. She was also a little old fashioned, so in her presence I curbed my desire to be in Lance's arms and kissing him with passion. We had a little Christmas celebration. I received a warm robe. I had brought perfume and cologne for the both of them. I was given Lance's childhood bedroom while he slept on the sofa in the living room. At night he would come to me and we would make fierce and passionate love. We made love on the floor by the fireplace, not far from his mother's room. After the lovemaking, we would talk softly, and it was on those nights that I learned that Lance had been married for two years, was separated and had a child by a college sweetheart. No love was involved, he said, as the girl tricked him into marriage. I was deeply hurt. Lance knew that I was getting a divorce from Scott. Before leaving Vermont, Lance and I went to the bank to retrieve the money I had sent him from Alaska. It was a tidy sum with the interest. Soon I was on the train returning to New York. Lance had promised he would come to visit me as soon as he could. New York was cold and covered with snow in the bleakness of January. I saw Andy and was happy that he looked well. He was expecting his appointment to Annapolis, which he himself secured with determination. When Lance came to see me, I painted his portrait in oil. I felt sad as I knew that this was the end of our romance and love. I couldn't see myself waiting for his eventual divorce and living the rest of my life in a small Vermont town.

My ambition was to be a great artist. I had left my sketching work at the restaurant and was now living in a fashionable neighborhood, Seventy-second Street and Lexington Avenue in Manhattan, in a lovely building, rather like a private home. The house had eight apartments and a superintendent or concierge. My unit had a room, kitchen and bathroom. The large room, both bedroom and sitting room, was dramatically painted in black, the kitchen crimson, in all a very theatrical effect with which I could envision my paintings on the walls. It was furnished sparingly with twin beds, a table, chairs and had a large closet in the hallway. The location was perfect for me near Fifth Avenue, and much less expensive than my studio apartment.

New York was an exciting place in those days. I was invited to various cocktail parties and met attractive men. Bob Banning was a male model in his 40s and very much heterosexual. We started to date. I had met him at the Harwyn Club, which catered to a lot of New York society. Bob took me on weekends to the Hamptons, to Connecticut. He was so suave and very expert. I was infatuated with him. Bob and I would often go to the Ember Club and also the Copacabana, near the Plaza Hotel. I went to gay bars, sometimes with Lyvia, where I would see some extraordinarily handsome young men. My thought at that time was, it is a shame that they are not attracted to women.

But New York was also a dangerous place. As I was walking one early evening on Park Avenue, I became aware of a Cadillac following me. I saw that an elderly man with gray hair was behind the wheel. He slowed down, smiling, opened his window and asked me if he could give me a ride home. I saw him sitting so benevolently and harmless looking that I quickly judged, a family man, returning home from his day of business. I acquiesced and as we sat and chatted in the front seat. He asked if he could offer me a drink at his home. As we came near Fifth Avenue, the man said he lived near by. At the time I was thinking, he is a single man, and perhaps living in the plush district, an art collector. We entered an elegant lobby and as we stepped into his apartment, the first thing I saw was a multitude of televisions, radios and various electrical appliances piled one on top of the other. I didn't need to see more as my inner voice told me better not ask any questions. After the drink I pretended to have a violent migraine headache, ran to the elevator, and into the streets. I hailed a taxicab for home. I was frightened; the man was obviously a fence for some burglars.

I was invited to many cocktail parties and made the acquaintance of a few interesting people. I jotted their names and phone numbers in a little black book. One afternoon as I entered my apartment, I saw that someone had been there. As I looked in the top drawer of a little desk where I kept some money and my black address book, both were missing. I immediately ran to the

visiting Mexico

superintendent of the building and told him. He said that nobody suspicious had entered the building and told me that I was the only one with the key. But I knew that he also had a passkey to all the apartments. I became uneasy and a little frightened. The next day I had a call from the district police station. I was to come down to the station that day. I remember the nice police officers. I spoke with a thick French accent. They were very kind and told me that they had found my leather bound black book and started to ask me questions. Apparently one of the names in the book was of a famous madam and they wanted to know if I had anything to do with her. I assured them that it was only a name that was given to me by a friend, and that I absolutely did not know the person. As the officers returned the book to me, I said that my apartment had been entered illegally and that money was missing. Also, I related my strange encounter with the man a couple of days previously and about the stolen goods. The policemen thanked me and said that they would take that man into custody.

I was disenchanted with New York and decided to take a trip to Mexico. So, with a sketchbook and a small suitcase, I arrived in Mexico City. In those days it was a bustling capital, crowded but not too smoggy. I found an inexpensive hotel in the Zona Rosa and started to tour the city. I went to Chapultepec Park, the museum, the floating gardens and saw the pyramids. At night I went dancing in a club called Jacaranda, where I met a charming man. He told me I must go to Taxco, that as an artist, I would find it inspiring. The next morning I took a bus and after a tiring journey arrived in a lovely setting in the mountains with a magnificent cathedral. I stayed a few days at Posada Mission and sketched the surrounding hills, the narrow streets and its people. While in Taxco I painted several watercolors. I met the muralist O'Gorman and his wife at the Posada. After a brief stay in Taxco and Cuernavaca, I returned to Mexico City. I had done many watercolors and I was proud of my collection of Mexican impressions.

One evening in a crowded restaurant as I was dining alone, I met a young consular attaché to the American embassy. His name was Russ Ambrose. I liked him and I began to see him often. He introduced me to the Director of the Mexican Tourist Bureau, Señor Villareal, to whom I showed the watercolors of my trip. He was very impressed and offered to give me an exhibit in the offices of the Tourism Bureau in Mexico City. So I had my work framed for that occasion. We had a champagne opening with many people, including press and television reporters, who were all very kind to this petite French artist. Russ was very proud of me. I was interviewed and the articles appeared in the Mexican newspapers. To celebrate my success, Russ had a surprise for me. We were to go spend a weekend in a small picturesque village called Tepototzlan a couple of hours from Mexico City.

Early the next morning, we left Mexico City and started our journey on a climbing dirt road. We passed many houses, shacks and primitive huts, pigs, small children, dirt and dust, some cactus, more hills and then a smooth narrow paved road, straight with no traffic. We made small talk. It was still early in the morning. Suddenly, we rear-ended a small stalled truck that seemed to appear from nowhere. I was sitting next to Russ, and my first reflex was to cover my face. In doing so, my elbow went through the windshield and I saw blood running on my arm. Russ was shaken and pale. I was crying with pain and in shock, very scared. We saw that the front of the car was totally demolished, the windshield shattered. After seeing that there were no injuries except for my bleeding elbow, we noticed that the truck with the Mexican driver had disappeared. We were alone, many miles from any house or town on this deserted road. Russ did everything to reassure me while I was crying and holding my bleeding arm. On the horizon we finally saw a black car appear. The four Mexicans stopped and quickly upon seeing the wreck, brought a bottle of whiskey and poured half of it on my arm to disinfect it. After that, we all piled in their car for the trip back to Mexico City. Those kind Mexican laborers left us at a medical clinic where I immediately went to be x-rayed. Fortunately, except for my arm bleeding, nothing was hurt.

After I healed and the exhibit was over at the Tourist Bureau, I left Mexico for Los Angeles. I took a taxi to Beverly Hills, where I consulted my address book so I could call my old friend from Cap d'Antibes, Osmanli Fariba. I settled in a small hotel behind the Beverly Wilshire Hotel, and called Osmanli. He was surprised to hear from me but very happy. He came to fetch me and I saw again my jolly, fat young friend. We had a lovely visit and I showed him my watercolor collection of Mexico. He was impressed and told me that my work was good. Forty years later that young man was to be a most respected French art dealer and collector in Paris. He became an owner of a vast collection of modern art.

Osmanli introduced me to many of his friends in Beverly Hills and Hollywood. I remember Lew Thorvik, a tall handsome Swede who was a journalist for the Hollywood foreign press. His twin brother was married and lived in a beautiful villa in the Hollywood hills. I dated Lew Thorvik and he liked me. He took me to glamorous places. Being a journalist with the foreign press, he knew a lot of movie actors and actresses. Once we went to a set to see the making of a film with Paul Newman and Joanne Woodward. Lew took me to dinner at Romanoff's, to Trader Vic's in Beverly Hills, and to the Biltmore Hotel to dine and dance. We would also dine at the Constellation in the Beverly Hilton, a lovely room done in white and gold where twenty romantic violins played for the patrons dining in candlelight softness. Lew was a gifted and sensual lover, and his apartment was decorated with erotica. I was flattered with his attention and he was most gallant. He would introduce me always as a famous French artist to his friends.

While I was staying in the small unpretentious hotel in Beverly Hills, I used to wander in the bigger hotel lobbies, looking at the people to study their expressions. I remember visiting the Beverly Wilshire, with its famous bar, Danny's Hydeaway, the Beverly Hilton, and the Beverly Hills Hotel, home of the famous Polo Lounge. I would gaze at the celebrities discreetly. A kind maître d' would speak French to me. I had a curvaceous figure and an enticing smile. Casually I would let him know that I was a friend of so and so. It would never fail, he would always find me a table in a crowded room.

One afternoon while I was sitting in the Beverly Hilton lobby, a young man approached me and said that he heard me speak French to one of the shop girls in the lobby store. He said he also was French and was the assistant manager of the hotel. We became friends through our mutual language and similar tastes. His name was Hervé Fayard and it was with Hervé that I first discovered Palm Springs during a weekend, when we drove to the desert. Palm Springs in the 1950's was an oasis, a small town, with a main street, few shops, lots of motels. We went to La Quinta and sat in the beautiful patio admiring the glorious sunset. The days were hot but the nights very cold. We went to see Twenty-Nine Palms and a couple of curio shops. Years later Hervé Fayard was to become the manager of the El Camino Real Hotel in Mexico City.

I had a letter of recommendation from Mr. Villareal from Mexico, to the Mexican Tourist Bureau in Beverly Hills. So I called Mr. Diego Zamora, the director, who was very cooperative on setting up an exhibit for me at the office of Mexican Tourism on Wilshire Boulevard to show my beautiful watercolors of Taxco, Cuernavaca, and Acapulco. The opening celebration for the exhibit was a success. All of my friends came as did friends of friends. Osmanli, the twins, Hervé, photographers, including the press for the Beverly Hills news, and many people I didn't know came to enjoy my exhibit. There were hors-d'oeuvres and drinks for the well-dressed guests. For my first show in America, I was elated as my work was well received.

After the show I returned to New York and tried to resume my life. I saw my brother Andy, who was in the navy, and soon became a midshipman at Annapolis Naval Academy. I decorated the apartment with masks that I had purchased in Mexico and put colorful blankets on the twin beds. But I was dissatisfied with and weary of New York. One day Lyvia called and asked me if I would like to join her to visit a friend in Dallas. I said yes, and a few days later we left for Texas.

I was not prepared for the vastness of the state of Texas. As we drove the long route from the airport, the heat engulfed us. We stayed in Lyvia's friend's apartment in a modern complex with a swimming pool. Every apartment had a patio and the evenings were balmy. I enjoyed the unexpected vacation and I was happy to be with Lyvia and her friends.

When, after two weeks, Lyvia had to return to New York to resume her work as interior decorator, I decided to stay in Dallas. I called on my one friend in Dallas and prayed that he remembered me. Bud Anson was pleased that I called him and came to see me at my friend's apartment. Soon we were together and Bud set me up in a residence hotel not far from his office. Dallas was a sprawling city, lots of land everywhere, big homes around Turtle Creek, wide streets, many apartment houses with pools. It was hot that early spring, hot and humid. The downtown area was expansive with big hotels, such as the Adolphus, the Hilton, and with many restaurants, bars and stores, including the prestigious Neiman Marcus, which covered a whole city block.

When time came to leave, I told Bud that I had to return to New York as I had been in Dallas a month and that my rent was due. Bud promptly told me not to worry, to let go of my place in New York and he would get me an apartment in Dallas. I never went back to New York after that, to live, and I never missed a thing I left in that apartment except for a few of my paintings. But I had my photographs, my Mexican watercolors and some clothes, and Bud was my friend and lover. I was set up in a very lovely apartment with modern furniture, a pool and a patio and Bud would visit me every day. He drank a lot but could hold his liquor. He was a stocky man and loved to drive his Cadillac. I was impressed with all his Texas wealth. We went to dine at the Chateau and at the Old Warsaw, some of the finest restaurants in Dallas. Bud was proud of me but also possessive. I was getting restless and weary of the fancy clubs and restaurants.

One day I told Bud that I would like to have a studio in which to paint. He told me that he had a vacant store that I could use as a studio. The place was located not far from a country club and across from a supermarket, laundromat and liquor store, and a small shopping area. My mind worked fast as I told Bud that I would open an art gallery. And that's how Gallery Vendome was born.

My idea was to promote Dallas artists while also displaying my own work. My watercolors of Mexico soon graced the walls of my new gallery, which also included watercolors of the famous Dallas artist Bud Biggs. The grand opening also showed artists like R. Mazza. After much effort and work, the gallery looked believable; it was small but artsy. The party was catered, with cocktails and wine. I had done some advertising in the local paper, the radio and TV. The opening was a success and I sold some of my watercolors. The Texans loved my French accent. I provided a guest address book for future reference for the next shows. I had thought of everything: logo for letterhead, envelopes, business cards. Everything was paid for by Bud but he was nowhere in sight. I could understand that he was proud of me, but he was a married man and I was his mistress. In those days, people were fairly puritanical. In a way he was protecting me. I was seeing less of him, but he was generous with money to buy clothes at Neiman Marcus and to cover the rent and the bills of the Gallery Vendome. Bud was a busy man. He was also a sportsman and he would take fishing trips to Alaska or go hunting in Canada. While he was on those trips, I dated other men and went to dine at the Cipango Club and the Adolphus Hotel. When Bud returned, I told him that I was working hard at the gallery everyday and I needed a vacation. I cajoled him into taking a trip to New Orleans. We left the next weekend and that trip was very enjoyable. We saw the French Quarter, dined at Antoine's, visited Bourbon Street, and the Artist Colony. Bud was a good companion but he would imbibe a lot and occasionally he was hard to handle. Nevertheless, I returned to Dallas happier.

Another month passed and Bud asked me to go with him on a fishing trip to Acapulco. We flew to Mexico from Dallas, from there we took a small plane to Acapulco. When we got out of the plane the air was hot and heavy with the scent of bougainvillea, frangipanis, hibiscus, palm trees, all so exotic. With the blue sea and azure skies, birds singing, I was intoxicated. The taxi came upon a lovely low building with private bungalows, Puerto Marques, where we were given a lovely room with a patio overlooking the ocean. I soon got my bikini on, and sat on the chaise lounge admiring the view. Bud got himself a drink, then another, and another and soon fell asleep snoring. I felt frustrated, I wanted to hear the mariachis and explore Acapulco Bay. But I had to be content to wait for the next day. Early morning, after a leisurely breakfast on the veranda we set out for the Club de Pesca. We hired a fishing boat with two sturdy young Mexican men and set out to sea. For an hour we struggled with our fishing rods, catching nothing. One of the men suddenly saw a big fish, caught it and the two of them with their bare hands brought an enormous fish onto the boat. The rest of the morning was leisurely and I was content to sunbathe. When we arrived at the pier, we all had our pictures taken with our catch. That night we went to see the divers, dined at Villa Vera and heard the mariachi band. Then, when the weekend ended, we flew back to Dallas.

Chapter Three

I RESUMED MY WORK at the Gallery Vendome. I was collecting a nice press book with photos and articles pertaining to my Dallas gallery and its shows of local artists. I started to work on a new one-man show for the French artist Robert Caron. I liked his work, delicate portraits in watercolors, reminiscent of Dufy's. Caron had several noted collectors in Texas and had exhibited in various country clubs around Dallas. His exhibit was successful. We had various newspaper articles in the local papers. We became friends and he painted a lovely portrait of me in shades of yellow, pink and blue, my favorite colors. Robert Caron invited me to visit him at his home in the South of France, which I did ten years later, with my son, then aged seven.

Bud would often go to Florida, where he had a winter home. One day we flew to Fort Lauderdale for a little vacation. We went fishing for marlin on Bud's boat, had cocktails and dinner at a seafood restaurant, and retired to the beach house. Invariably Bud had too much to drink and always fell asleep while attempting to make love. I would then move to the other twin bed. But in the middle of the night, Bud was again on top of me. Bud was generous yet childish in a strange way, so I gave in, tried to please him.

I was putting some money in the bank. I had been in Dallas almost a year and it was now Christmas time. I called Andy and asked him to come celebrate the holidays with me. He was now in Annapolis, Maryland. It was good to see my brother, very handsome in his midshipman's uniform, navy blue with a white visored cap. We had dinner at Restaurant Chateaubriand. Bud and Andy got along well. On New Year's Day we went to the Big Game of Army-Navy, and I had a nice party for Andy that evening, with Bud, my French girlfriend Colette who came to visit me from Cannes, and a couple from Scottsdale, who lived in the next apartment. We drank champagne, took pictures, and had a pleasant time ushering in 1956.

I heard from time to time from the attorney, but I made no hasty decisions regarding my divorce. I got letters from Miles, with whom I was correspond-ing. In the last one he announced his divorce from his Romanian wife. He also said that he missed me and, if I came back to San Francisco, he had plans for me. Although Bud was proud of my work at the gallery, sometimes I saw myself going nowhere. My biological clock was ticking; I wanted marriage, children. To be honest with myself, being the mistress of a married man was not my ideal. I first had to get a divorce, by establishing residence in Nevada for five weeks and filing the papers. After the holidays I moved to a small apartment near the gallery. I didn't miss the pool and was busy with promo-tion of the gallery. Bud was getting jealous of my friends and would often get drunk. We had words and I told him I wanted to leave Dallas.

The next time I saw Bud, after refusing to see him for a few weeks, he had airplane tickets. We were to go to the Virgin Islands and San Juan, Puerto Rico on a vacation. Going away might help me to see with clarity what I wanted in life. The Caribbean was beautiful: the island of St. Thomas, with its beaches, the flowers, the aquamarine water, the flamboyant exotic trees. San Juan, with its rhythms, the casinos. I felt more relaxed in the warm sun and let myself go in those few languid days. Bud was kind and while we returned to Dallas on a small plane, I saw myself clutching at his arm for reas-surance and comfort.

As I was thinking more of my future, I only saw two alternatives. Staying, I would need money to improve the gallery, to keep in competition with the ones in the new shopping center a few miles away. That meant to ask Bud, and bind me more, obligate me, and to make a commitment to Dallas, which in the final analysis, I found to be too provincial. So I opted to pack my little suitcase and go to Las Vegas. It may have been a hasty decision, but I had to be true to my nature. So I parted with Bud, left the apartment, closed the gallery, and wrote Miles that I was on my way to Las Vegas to get my divorce.

When I returned to Dallas ten years later, Bud's wife had died. He, still alcoholic, was living in his big house, with only a housekeeper. I visited him. I had been divorced from Miles and had a seven-year-old son. I was glad that I had not stayed in Dallas, and for the second time parted with no regrets.

I arrived in Las Vegas and found an apartment near the Sahara Hotel Casino and paid a month's rent. I sent a letter to the attorney telling him I had taken residency in Nevada. The apartment was luxurious and expensive and I needed money, so remembering the contract I had, I contacted Hunt Albanese, the owner of the El Rancho Vegas Hotel. He remembered me and told me that I could do my portrait sketches in the lounge. I worked the lounges, while wearing my artsy costumes and did portraits of casino customers. I came home in the evenings with a purse heavy with silver dollars. I explored the hotel casinos, the Flamingo Hotel, the lounge at the Sands, the Dunes Casino. It was a great time, very glamorous!

I called Miles and told him I was looking forward to seeing him. Unexpectedly, he came from San Francisco to Las Vegas one weekend. We had a romantic time and I remember the sandstorms in the desert. The first one, sand everywhere, under doors, it came through windows. We had sand in our eyes and on our lips. I was wearing a pink and blue dress and Miles and I took pictures on the small balcony of the apartment. Miles left and now I was sure of my feelings for him. So, when I finally received my divorce paper from the attorney, I left Las Vegas, for San Francisco. I was a free woman. Miles was waiting for me at the San Francisco airport with his little red Corvette and we proceeded to his home.

The first few days were romantic and we were making plans for our future together. We visited some of Miles' friends, who found me charming and told Miles that he was indeed a lucky man. I met Miles' parents. His mother, Lillian Sherwyn, was a medium-size woman, blond, in her early fifties. She had a girlish laugh and adored her only son. His father, Sam, a professional man, was kind and they welcomed this petite French girl into the family.

We had a civil wedding in San Francisco performed by a judge, a distant cousin of the family. Miles and I flew to Hawaii for our honeymoon. We explored the islands, and swam. We both got deep tans, wore colorful Hawaiian clothes, attended a festive luau, danced hula dances, and took a lot of pictures for memories. Miles and I walked the beach and listened to the soft sounds of the waves. It was so romantic. We made love to the music of ukuleles coming from under our window, near the Banyan tree at the Ala Moana. To prolong the honeymoon, we decided to take the boat back to San Francisco. So we booked the trip on the ship *Matsonia*, for five glorious days at sea. We made friends on that journey. Miles and I were popular, as honeymooners always seem to be. An elderly lady and her much younger escort intrigued us. We soon sat together at cocktail time, telling jokes and stories. Miles was a good raconteur. At night in our small but comfortable cabin, we made fierce love. I think our son was conceived on that trip. The seas were calm as we returned home to San Francisco and I was as content as any young bride. We saw Miles' parents every week. Soon I realized I was pregnant and we were all overjoyed.

Miles was working as a real estate salesman and would leave early in the morning for the office. I would call his mother, who was very kind and happy at the prospect of becoming a grandmother. We shopped in downtown San Francisco for maternity clothes and lunched at Blum's or Townsend's. The house we lived in was a modest tract home, but to me everything was luxury: the large spacious kitchen with the pastel matching stove and refrigerator, the tile floor, the two large bedrooms. The small den I selected as the baby's room and I decorated it in pale yellow. We did not know the gender of our baby, but I was almost positive it would be a boy.

Miles and I went often to dine and dance at the Fairmont Hotel, Alexis, Le Trianon and, of course, Vanessi's. Cocktails in the Cirque Room would often end with dinner and dancing at the Presidio Officers' Club with our friends Colonel Bill and Lottie Randall. Lottie was French and had been a friend of Miles and his ex-wife. She and her husband remained friendly with Miles after his divorce. Lottie and I spoke French together. We liked each other. Miles and Bill got on well. One Saturday night at a dinner-dance at the Presidio, I was dancing with Bill. I was eight months pregnant and wearing a black chiffon dress. I was having difficulty walking, much less dancing, but I was at peace with myself, awaiting the birth of my baby.

The doctor said that it was not uncommon for a first child to be late. Finally, on the ninth day past my due date, I was delivered of a healthy boy. I was overjoyed with pride and happiness. In retrospect, the happiest time of my life up to then was the eight days I spent in the hospital with all the attention of my in-laws and my husband, and the caring hospital staff.

I remember the ride home in the red Corvette with my new son in my arms, wrapped in white silk, with only his small pink face showing. The house was cheerful with lots of flowers. The mother's helper was already there to attend to my needs so I could take care of my newborn. Lillian, the new grandmother, was there to nurture me. It was the American dream, cozy and perfect. Next came the neighbors' attentions with small gifts or greeting cards. Soon I was sending birth notices and thank you notes to friends and relatives on both sides of the ocean. Life would never be the same now for me. I was nursing the baby and getting up every two hours at night the first two weeks. I became nervous as Miles would stay later and later at work. I was becoming worried, perhaps unduly. So, after two months I gave the baby a bottle. Miles and I decided to get help, so we hired a Swiss au pair girl. It worked fine and when little Gregory, Gregg for short, was five months old and thriving, I decided that I would return to work at Bimbo's.

I was welcomed once again. The working hours suited me well, from eight o'clock in the evening to two o'clock in the morning. That gave me afternoons with my little son, while the au pair girl took care of him in the mornings and I slept until noon. Then I would take over. I would cook an early dinner and Miles would drive me to the club. He would return to fetch me at closing time and we went home.

One afternoon I ventured into a tailor shop located on Geary Boulevard. I had heard some classical music, Mozart! A man was sitting behind a counter sewing, smiling at me. I noticed some original oil paintings on the walls. His name was Martyn Bresnick, he was European, and was interested in art and artists. We became friends and soon after that he arranged a small exhibit of my sketches in his tailor shop cum art gallery. Martyn, later introduced me to Benny Bufano, a famous San Francisco sculptor, who was to have a strong influence in my life.

Often, while Miles was waiting for me to finish my work at Bimbo's, he would come with alcohol on his breath and sit and drink in the bar. Sometimes I worried about the safety of his driving us home. After six months of this pattern, I left Bimbo's to stay home and paint, and to take care of Gregg, who was now a year old. My brother Andy had graduated from the Naval Academy and was now a lieutenant stationed at Hamilton Air Force Base just north of San Francisco. We enjoyed having him stay with us in our guest room. Two years later, Andy met Ingrid, a lovely Scandinavian stewardess, and fell in love. They eloped and got settled in an apartment in Sausalito.

Spring was warm that year, and I would often take Gregg to Golden Gate Park with Lillian. But I soon wearied of housework, cooking, cleaning, and the discord with Miles. My dreams of becoming a serious artist were still with me, but I lacked organization and could not concentrate. Miles would often stay two or more days away on business trips and that made me feel insecure. I needed reassurance in my new life and Miles was very immature and impatient. Tension arose. Lillian was very understanding as she was the only person I could turn to. But naturally she was partial to the son whom she adored.

I arranged an area in which to paint in the garage of our home and enrolled in the Art Academy. A few hours a week I took classes and painted. My first instructor was Lundy Siegriest, the painter, and son of Louis Siegriest. I was very interested in the different styles but I gravitated toward expressionism and the use of many colors. I brought home my first oil painting which was like a sun burst, a rather modern interpretation. Miles was not impressed, which hurt me deeply, as I had favorable comments at class from the teacher and students alike. Miles' drinking pattern continued and we had more arguments and fights. I decided to stay away from him for awhile, so I packed up little Gregg, a few belongings, and stayed at a friend's home.

After awhile, under the influence of Lillian, I returned, but Miles' negative behavior did not improve. After separating a second time, my friends advised me to seek a lawyer. I had been married four years and saw no future with Miles. I was not interested in staying and keeping the house. All I asked was to keep my son and receive adequate child support. Miles was vindictive and bitter, I was very hurt, and so were his parents, Lillian and Sam. After waiting a year, we were finally divorced. Miles was allowed visitation rights with his son and I received a small allowance for child support. But I was relieved and not at all afraid to start anew.

I moved out of the house with the furniture and found a large unfurnished flat in the Richmond District, on a quiet avenue near Golden Gate Park. It was sunny and light and accessible to all parts of the city by public transportation. I resumed portrait work, to supplement my meager income. The next thing for me was to find a baby-sitter for evenings, so I placed an ad in the newspaper and hired a pleasant, middle-aged woman. She stayed with us in the guest bedroom and took charge of Gregg in the evenings.

I went to the newly built San Francisco Hilton downtown and presented myself to the assistant manager for work. After a favorable interview, I was assigned a small space in an alcove near the coffee shop and opposite the cocktail lounge in the hotel lobby. So I brought in my easel and paper and charcoal to do patrons' portraits. While I was eager, I did well, but the pace was too slow and the hotel was new. As I was looking for an alternative, I heard of a position at the Domino Club downtown in the financial district, where I would sketch nude models with another artist, Roberto Lupetti. That lasted a couple of months; then I checked into some other places, some other clubs.

I was now working steadily at a Broadway supper club called Goman's Gay Nineties, located on the Barbary Coast. The club was done in plush red velvets. The rococo decor was turn of the century San Francisco, complete with a large bar and dining room. In the cheerful lounge a pianist played old songs while customers would sing along. I enjoyed working in that atmosphere. From the main room could be heard laughter and music and singing as the Goman family was doing its vaudeville acts. I wore a turn-of-the-century costume, a short corset with flowers and low-cut bustier, with black stockings and high heels. I carried my sketchpad and crayons as I strolled among the patrons. It was a good job and I was making decent money. I acquired a lot of polish and savoir faire at Goman's. But working in the proximity of gaudy Broadway was unpleasant and often after work I would take a taxi home, to be safe.

Little Gregg was the joy of my life. During the day we would go to the zoo with Lillian, or to San Mateo park to picnic, or at the Marina Green just to sunbathe and play. Miles would see him on visitation days but most of the time, Lillian would take little Gregg for the weekend.

At the end of that year, I left Goman's to work at a club on Nob Hill, called The Interlude. I was one of two artists sharing the spotlight with a nude model. It was artsy, like the Domino, and the ambiance was fun and relaxed. It was also very good practice for me, as I had stopped going to the Art Academy. Between the three or four shows in the evenings, I would sketch portraits of the patrons and make extra money. My work there only lasted a short time. But I had met a wonderful lady friend who, with her small daughter, would vacation in Tahoe with little Gregg and me.

My next work place was very much to my liking. It was in downtown San Francisco on Sutter Street, an Asian nightclub-restaurant called The Forbidden City. After climbing a flight of stairs patrons entered a large foyer and bar decorated in Oriental motifs. Girls dressed in cheong san gowns slit to the waist were serving drinks. The lovely oval-eyed proprietress had me contribute a reasonable percentage of my tips for the privilege of working in the club. I wore a Chinese smock with a high collar, of yellow gold silk, black fishnet stockings, and again high heel shoes. Coby Yee and Charlie Low were wonderful people. Their nightclub revue was risqué but in good taste. I liked the production, the music, the acts, with very talented young Chinese and Japanese singers and dancers. The nightclub was full on most weekends.

During the day I wandered into Perry's on Union Street, then just becoming a new artsy neighborhood. I enjoyed visiting the Artist Cooperative Gallery, which catered to local artists, to view their art and the various esthetic trends. At the Art Academy I had studied with Lundy Siegriest and I now favored a post-impressionist style. I longed to have a studio of my own, a real inspirational place to paint. But I had to content myself with my work at The Forbidden City, sketching portraits, always using the same technique, gray charcoal paper, with black and white conté crayons for highlights.

My friend Martyn had closed the tailor shop and opened an art gallery, and I visited him often in his new gallery on Sutter Street. He gave me courage;

when I brought him some paintings, he would always buy a few. Among his first purchases were my self-portrait done in my first studio in Manhattan and the bullfight sketches in black and white done in Mexico City. Gregg was thriving as a delightfully mischievous and sturdy six-year-old boy. It was at that time that I went to work in my last nightclub, having left the Forbidden City.

The Gold Dust was a trendy club, located opposite the fashionable Playboy Club of San Francisco in an alley near Sansome Street. It also had turn-of-the-century decor, all in red velvet, with a large bar. The mezzanine was set with tables and in the middle a swing was suspended from the ceiling. During the shows, a lovely nude woman was spotlighted as she swayed to and fro on the swing. The clients of the Gold Dust were family men, lawyers, stock brokers, and office workers who would come for cocktails from the Financial District. The club was very dim and I often had to strain my eyes to see the faces I was sketching. The absence of light could eventually affect my vision and I was naturally concerned. One night, a very distinguished-looking gentleman let me sketch his portrait. After a few minutes, I handed him the finished work, which he examined carefully. He then asked me if I would like to make an attractive sum of money by using my artistic talents. He commissioned me to sketch in pen and ink a series of nude positions of explicit lovemaking and sexual acts between a man and a woman. I was not offended at the strange request as I considered nude drawings artistic, but he wanted graphic drawings. He returned a few days later and I handed him my work, which was artistically tasteful. He was satisfied and gave me a generous check. I felt a little guilty afterwards, but then it was a commissioned work, albeit a strange one.

One day, while walking along Washington Square, I saw in the window of a real estate office a sign advertising a house for rent in the Marina District. A charming old Italian man offered to show me the place. It was a one-story flat, located a few blocks from the Palace of Fine Arts. I moved from the Avenues, to the spacious and airy flat. It had two bedrooms, a sun-porch, a large living room with a fireplace, a dining room, and a bright, spacious kitchen. Gregg went to a nearby elementary school, Winfield Scott. I liked the Mediterranean look of the houses on Marina Boulevard and the quiet, provincial Chestnut Street.

I resumed my work but I was looking at new ventures. One afternoon, as I was browsing on Broadway, I came upon an antique shop. I asked the young man in charge if he knew of any space or studio for rent. We became friends and soon I found myself sharing a spacious room upstairs with Lorenzo

Antiques Boutique. I named my place Alexandra Gallery. I needed paintings to fill the walls so I went to the Artists' Cooperative to seek talented local artists. My first exhibit attracted a lot of people. The paintings were colorful and varied. I had about five or six artists represented, including some of my works. The San Francisco crowd included art critics, newspapermen, and photographers. I was thrilled that my brother Andy came to share in my first opening.

To access the gallery clients had to climb a flight of stairs, then cross a small patio that backed up to a sheer cliff that was lit up at night. It was striking. Near the new gallery was a Chinese grocer and the famous restaurant Vanessi. On the other side of the street was the bar El Matador, run by Barnaby Conrad and in between the bar and the gallery was Walter Keane's studio. Walter and I were friends and I received his best wishes for the opening of Alexandra's Gallery. I went to Vanessi's often for lunch and to visit my friend, the genial host Bart Shea, who put many of my works on the walls of his restaurant.

Among the gallery's many visitors who signed my guest book were Herb Caen, the art dealer Cory, and other celebrities. I acquired a thick scrapbook of photos, articles, and writeups. One photo that I still have was of the famous lawyer, Jack Erlich. I did his portrait and he kindly dedicated a large photo of himself to me. I remember going to Jack's Restaurant in San Francisco, where he always had his table and I was a frequent guest at lunch. Also at that period I went often to Enrico's sidewalk café, where I would chat with owner Enrico Banducci. I would go to the Hungry I to see the shows and to the Vesuvio Café. I was very nostalgic for France.

The paintings sold well during the first few months. Lorenzo and Tom would help with sales as they had the antique shop across the patio. I dated sometimes but I wasn't interested in anyone in particular. My little son occupied all my leisure time. After a young, but very gifted, artist named Dario came to the gallery for me to view his work, I decided to give him a one-man show. He was an excellent realist painter, and Lorenzo and I agreed that we should have a grand opening. Dario had many friends and also knew collectors. The exhibit cocktail party was glamorous, with lots of well-dressed people. My outfit was of pale blue crepe de chine dress and I had a smart hairdo.

I visited Martyn's often and one day as I came by his gallery on Sutter Street, he introduced me to a small man with grayish hair and confident visionary eyes, clear and penetrating. It was my first encounter with the famous controversial sculptor, Benny Bufano, who later invited me to visit

"the imaginative flight
reaching to Touch every shores
on earth and all space."

quote: Bufano

him in his studio on Minna Street. Martyn commented on my artistic talents and Benny, as he was called, was gallant with me. We spoke Italian and a little French. I later became very acquainted with his work. After Dario's show, business began to deteriorate. The economy had been slow ever since President Kennedy's assassination. After managing the gallery for eighteen months, I told Lorenzo that I had to give up the lease. I wasn't going to persevere as the gallery was too confining. My gypsy spirit was longing to take flight. I needed new horizons and was homesick for France. I had saved some money and in the late spring of 1967 when Gregg had just turned seven years old, I booked passage on a ship, the SS *Constitution*, from New York to Cannes for a two-week cruise. Before I left for France I sublet the flat to three nurses; this later proved disastrous. My adorable, mischievous son—who had a full head of sandy-colored hair—and I flew to New York.

On board the ship we had a small but cozy cabin. The leisurely days were spent on deck by the pool with the other passengers. We hit port every two or three days, so no one had time to really get acquainted. In the first port of Lisbon we visited the old city, including the antique quarter with its steep stairs and glorious views. Next we went to Gibraltar with the impressive Rock. Then on to the island of Madera, although we did not go ashore, something I regret to this day. The ship sailed to the beautiful bay of Naples, Italy where the climate was hot, the sky so blue. Gregg and I took a horse and buggy ride, near Santa Lucia, but the city was dirty, something I had not noticed when I was there for my first visit with Brent Fletcher, when we were so in love.

Now I was a simple tourist. As the ship sailed, I found myself often sketching the view from aboard it. Invariably, a small group of fellow passengers peered over my shoulder and commented on my talents and wished they could do the same. Next we came to the charming, picturesque port of Portofino with houses of red and yellow, all in the Mediterranean style; the terrace cafés were full of people eating, drinking and mingling joyously. I am back in Europe again, I was thinking, as Gregg and I sat with cold drinks on a terrace. Next stop was to be Cannes. I had come full circle.

In Cannes, we left the SS Constitution, and at last I had come home from where I had started, and I was with my son. Cannes had changed very little. With renewed pleasure I saw the shapes of the hills of the Esterel mountains, the harbor of Cannes, and the old Suquet. I was able to locate the woman who was my witness at my wedding to Scott. She had several profitable businesses, including a laundry shop. She told me that she would be willing to rent me a small apartment near the beach for the month of July, the height of the season. The price was very high but the apartment was clean and had a kitchen. It was better than being at a hotel. Cannes in those days was very style conscious, and I had brought with me three suitcases of beautiful dresses.

The first couple of weeks were wonderful. Little Gregg and I swam in the blue Mediterranean. We took trains to visit the small towns I knew so well on the French Riviera, and went to the marketplaces to buy fresh food. Gregg was never without a small bottle of drinking water as he wouldn't drink water from the tap, which was just as well. One day I called upon my artist friend Robert Caron, who lived in the old town of St. Cezaire. He was happy to hear from me, remembering me from Dallas. He invited us to visit him. We took a bus and after an hour or so of climbing a hill, it arrived in his old village. Robert, in sandals and a large straw hat, was there to greet us. We drove some more miles to arrive in a "Mas Provençal" with large sandy-colored stones from Provence, lots of cypress trees shading the courtyard, and a swimming pool. The weather was hot. Robert showed us our room. Our visit was a few short days. Then we all sat outside and had a cold drink, talked and reminisced of Texas. Robert Caron had aged; he now had grayish hair and a smart mustache. I wanted to see his new work so he said later, he would show me his studio, which was detached from the main house. It had been about ten years since we last saw each other. I had blossomed with motherhood and Robert had a glint of desire in his eyes. In true Gaelic manner, Robert's demeanor was flattering as he showed me through his home. I related to Robert all about my recent venture, the now closed gallery in San Francisco. I told him that I was not planning much, except a wonderful vacation of three months in Europe. Before leaving, we took many photos by the swimming pool and Robert promised to visit us in Cannes. When the weekend drew to a close, Gregg and I returned to Cannes.

On the Carlton Beach where we always went for swimming, I met a charming couple from New York, Irina and Seymour Babcock. Sey was a top executive for a television station. They lived in a fashionable apartment near Central Park. They invited little Gregg and me for a boat ride to Cap d'Antibes and then to lunch, where we took many photos. A few years after that, on a visit to New York, I called upon Sey and Irina and brought a painting as a gift. Unfortunately their marriage had dissolved by that time. Sey had been courting me discreetly in Cannes. In New York we had a brief affair. We liked each other, but lived far apart. During that period I saw Jasper Markham at the Pierre Hotel in Manhattan.

That year I looked exceptionally good in Cannes, just thirty-seven years old, slim, tan, with a voluptuous bosom. I felt confident even while wearing a tiny bikini and playing on the beach with my little son. One evening in the middle of July, I sat at the terrace of the Carlton Hotel and wore an elegant red velvet dress, with an open back and two tiny rows of rhinestones criss-crossing the waist. A gentleman got up and came to my table and politely invited me to sit with his small group. After a glass of champagne we left to dine at La Poele d' Or, a fine restaurant. Then we went to the Palm Beach Casino that I revisited now in style. Hubert, my new friend, put a thousand dollars worth of chips in front of me at the baccarat table. I knew very little about how to play, as my favorite games were "trente et quarante" and roulette. While he was busy at another table, I put half of the chips in my small evening bag to be cashed the next day and, of course, I lost the rest. I thought that the money I secreted would pay for the rent on the apartment as my money was dwindling rapidly in expensive Cannes that summer. Hubert was very nice, a quiet man. We saw each other on two other occasions when he took Gregg and me to lunch at the Palm Beach by the pool. Then he left and I never saw him again. It was difficult to entertain with a young boy, but my priority was to my son. I wanted to give him the best of times on this trip. I needed my son's affection more than I needed a relationship.

The month of July drew to a close and I purchased bus tickets for Gregg and me to take the scenic route to Geneva, Switzerland, by the Route Napoleon. We rode in the comfortable high bus to small towns such as Castellane up in the hills, through the rocky mountain passes to Annecy and Grenoble, finally arriving in Geneva with its lovely lake. We stayed there a few days to tour the lake. Then we took a small train to Gstaad, to the Palace Hotel, Montreux, Lausanne. Gregg enjoyed it all, the French croissants so flaky and delicious, the tasty fruits and food, all new to him. He learned a few words of French besides the ones I had taught him. Then we took a train to Paris. At last I was seeing the capital, after so many years. It was a long time indeed. Ten years.

Seeing Paris again was wonderful. We stayed in a small hotel on Avenue Victor Hugo near Etoile and the Champs Elysées. The hotel belonged to the Egbergs, an elderly couple who were once cooks at the orphanage Malmaison. They owned the hotel but during the war it had been requisitioned by the Germans. After the war, the Egbergs had returned to their hotel, repaired it, and reopened for business. Gregg and I had a comfortable room with a private shower and a balcony overlooking the Arch de Triomph. During the day we strolled through the familiar districts I had known in my youth. As I introduced my son to Luxembourg Gardens, Saint Germain, Montparnasse, the Champs Elysées, the rue de Rivoli, the Palais Royal, we wore our shoes out. I had a distant cousin, an old maid, whom we visited. Over tea in her small apartment, she told me that since we were going to England on our next stop, we should visit our relatives there, also second cousins.

The month of August was very hot. One afternoon Gregg and I were sipping cold drinks and sitting in the terrace of Café de la Paix, Place de l' Opera. Paris in August was full of tourists. Most Parisians, to escape the heat, evacuate to the south of France or Normandy. Two men sitting nearby us were speaking Portuguese. I don't recall who started the conversation, but soon we were talking together, half Spanish and half French. They were curious, as I was speaking English to the boy and French to the waiter. Both men were Brazilian, tourists from Sao Paulo traveling for the first time in Paris. That evening they invited Gregg and me to dine on the Bateau Mouche and to see the illuminated splendor of Paris monuments by night. Later we went to Montmartre to see the artists at work. Both men were impressed when I told them I had started my career as an artist there. I kept their addresses in my book. Years later, while I was working as an art instructor on a ship cruising around South America, Gregg, who was on the cruise with me, and I visited Sao Paulo and called upon my Brazilian friend Alonzo. The three of us had a lovely lunch at Torre d' Italia.

London was gray and foggy. We found a small pension in Kensington. My first call was to my cousin Michael and his wife, who lived in a suburb of London called Finchley. I was the daughter of Shimon, his father's brother. They met us at the station. They asked several questions and were overjoyed that they had American cousins. The dinner was delicious ethnic food. I discovered that I had many cousins. The family consisted of six sisters and two brothers, all married with families of their own. I saw many relatives of all generations at that meeting. They were affectionate and kind to Gregg and me. I wondered, "What would have become of me, if I had gone to England instead of America?" After those long years, I had found a family, my English family.

Gregg and I resumed our tour of London with a visit to the British Museum, the London Bridge, the infamous Tower, and Buckingham Palace with its changing of the Guard, which delighted little Gregg. I took lots of pictures of the Crown Jewels, Soho, the Thames River, Chelsea, Bond Street, Picadilly Circus, and the department stores: Harrod's, Selfridges, Marks and Spencer. We had tea in an English teahouse and then it was time to come home. Our three-month trip had ended. We flew from Gatwick airport directly to San Francisco.

Gregg was very happy to see his father and grandparents again. It was after that trip to Europe that I decided to send Gregg to a military academy at Palo Alto, just after his eighth birthday. That first exciting trip to Europe made me realize that it was not being an artist in nightclubs or a gallery owner that I wanted out of life. But truly, in adjusting my priorities now with the vision to my future, I wanted to travel and paint. The two desires united, not to be confined but to seek different horizons, cultures, the excitement of new places, faces, exotic lands and inspiration for painting. The Marina flat seemed small and my life dull and domestic. While thinking of a way to combine my talents and remembering the interest of the passengers on the cruise ship about my drawing, the idea came to my mind, to utilize my talents to seek a position aboard one of the many cruise lines that came to San Francisco. I endeavored to write a resume offering, in addition to giving art classes and lessons, to teach French, Spanish, Russian, Italian, and Polish, languages I spoke. This could be my ticket around the world. I composed a resume, rewriting it many times, and found the courage to send it to a few of the cruise ship companies.

That winter was very quiet. In the spring of 1968, Gregg entered the military academy in Palo Alto. In the preceding months his grandmother and I were busy outfitting him with his little uniforms, khaki, blues, sport clothes, shoes, all labeled with his name. The academy was very pleasant, with large white buildings shaded by cool trees in a quiet part of Palo Alto, a lovely town near Stanford University. The parade grounds and classroom buildings were all extremely clean, well kept, as were the cadets' rooms, which were shared two boys to a room. Gregg looked a little scared and my heart melted at seeing my little boy living among other boys his age and older cadets. Gregg looked so young, so tender. But I quickly dismissed those thoughts and I said to myself it was for his own good, to be raised and trained to become a self-sufficient and disciplined man, to have male examples. I had become so attached to my son. He didn't see his father frequently and Miles was dissipating rapidly. Gregg was able to come home on weekends. Alternate weekends he would be picked up by his grandparents.

Of my several proposals to cruise companies, two sent replies. One was from the British company P. O. Lines which offered me a three week cruise to the Caribbean in exchange for art lessons. The other letter was a request for an interview with the director of shipboard personnel of the American

President Lines of San Francisco, Harlan Burke. I replied immediately and presented myself at the office near the shipping terminal Pier 32. Mr. Burke was a pleasant, rotund man with white hair and a pink, jovial face. He was impressed with my resume. I had also added in the resume such talents, all feigned, as yoga teacher, palm reader, cosmetologist, and art lecturer, in addition to my aforementioned abilities, as an artist and instructor of multiple languages. (When I worked on a Black Sea cruise, my Russian proved to be useful, in the port of Odessa.)

The interview with Mr. Burke was favorable but I had yet to meet Wade Rudiger, the ship's cruise director and chief purser. The position for which I was interviewed was to join the ship on her 'round-the-world cruise in the fall of 1968. When I had my first interview with Mr. Rudiger, I was nervous. After questioning me at great length, and being noncommittal, he told me that I would be advised by mail. The wait was long. Several times I telephoned Mr. Burke, who was always cordial. Finally, in the middle of August, I received a formal letter of acceptance. I was to be the art and language instructor on the ship *President Roosevelt*, leaving at the end of October for her trip around the world for ninety days. In exchange I would get a state cabin, passage, and gratuities for my room steward and waiter in the dining room. An addendum for the purchase of all art materials and language books required me to see the ship's purchasing agent as soon as possible. I was elated by the news. The following week, at a meeting in Mr. Burke's office, I gave him my list of materials, easels, watercolors, brushes, paper, mats for framing, charcoal. I wrote a general outline of my program at sea. I would teach from still life, taking into consideration that we were on a ship. Watercolor seemed a good choice. We had to store the easels for exhibits. I also made the mention of the French Made Simple teaching books and the English/Spanish and English/Russian books. I went then to the purchasing agent and gave him the estimate. My supply requisition was approved. I also signed a merchant marine document to make my position as art teacher and language intructor official with the American President Lines.

The time came for me to finish my packing. I hugged my little boy and kissed him tenderly, telling him to be very good, and careful. I paid the three month's rent for the flat and the semester tuition at the academy for Gregg. It left me with very little money in the bank, but I was confident that at the end of the trip around the world, I would be enriched and perhaps even sell a few paintings during the voyage. The day of sailing came and grandmother and Gregg saw me off. I tried to smile but I was a little sad, also. I had never left my son for such a long time. But now after our last embrace and kiss, and with many recommendations, I boarded the *President Roosevelt* and it sailed from Pier Thirty-Two, amidst streamers, confetti, and music. It was a joyous affair with people lined several deep to wish their friends and relatives bon voyage. The sirens whistled and the band played. The sky was a lovely blue, the air balmy. Indian summer had just begun in San Francisco. As I looked around the deck, I saw many older couples, small groups of elderly ladies but only a few young couples. The small groups of ladies waved their handkerchiefs in the wind to their loved ones on the pier.

Our first port of call was Honolulu, Hawaii, a five-day journey from San Francisco. On this first trip everything was new and strange to me on this 'round-the-world voyage, which proved to be an strange experience on this, my first trip. The SS *President Roosevelt* was a medium sized ship in the American President Line fleet, which also counted the twin ships President Cleveland and President Wilson, both smaller ships. On them the passengers numbered five hundred maximum and an equal crew number. But the Roosevelt carried even less, around three hundred and sixty passengers on their 'round-the-world voyage. Some passengers would disembark at various ports and the ship would also pick up passengers at other ports. My cabin was very comfortable; with a porthole, a bunk bed, private shower and toilet with a basin and mirror above, and a small double closet for clothes. The empty suitcases were left outside the cabin to be stored away. Earlier I had inventoried the art materials on the pier before they were put in storage, to the attention of the cruise director and chief purser, Mr. Rudiger. After we passed under the Golden Gate Bridge, which was for me an unusual experience, I went down to my cabin to unpack a few clothes. I proceeded to the purser's desk to register as we were told to do and into the dining room to get my table assignment. The chief steward was a large man and very friendly. He told me we would have open seating until we left Honolulu. Then I would be assigned my own table, a privilege of a staff member. I didn't know any of the other members of the staff, but as I glanced at the daily journal posted by the purser's office, I saw that we had a meeting that first day at 2 P.M. in the main lounge. I would have a chance to meet all the people I was to work with, for the next ninety days. I was very excited and a bit apprehensive.

I went to the bar, which was already filled with people sitting on stools. Around small, well-anchored tables, a waiter was busy serving drinks. It was eleven o'clock in the morning. A man with confetti in his hair smiled at me and I felt a little reassured. After a bit of small talk he introduced me to his table companions as the cruise art teacher and instructor of languages. After accepting their offers of a drink, I wandered up on deck again. People were standing against the railing watching the ocean, and far off on the horizon, diminishing rapidly, the lovely skyline of San Francisco. The air was fresh and a cool breeze began to blow. Small groups of passengers went to their cabins to unpack and get ready for lunch in the dining room on A Deck. I had a fair orientation of the ship by now, but I could still get lost easily. A young waiter was sounding the bell chimes to summon passengers for the first seating. I chose to wait for the second seating and explore more of the ship.

My feet were hurting as I still had on my high heels. I was wearing a light beige dress and an orange silk scarf that day. I went down to my cabin again to change shoes and I noticed under my door was the journal for the day. I resolved to see the print shop. As I passed the purser's office, I came upon the photo shop where a small man in his early fifties, neat in a khaki shirt and dark trousers, was unlocking the door. I introduced myself to him. His name was Kyle Harris, the ship's photographer. He said he had taken some photos of me on deck, as I waved goodbye to my son and Lillian. He noticed I was a little anxious and said not to be too concerned about Mr. Rudiger, the chief purser, as he was a somewhat gruff but good man. Kyle was my first friend on the ship. Kyle reminded me of the staff meeting that afternoon and cautioned me not to be late.

I went to the dining room and selected a table with three ladies, all very grandmotherly. I smiled and we talked. I had my first of many enjoyable meals on board. The dining room was cheerful, with white table cloths, and silverware. The attentive young waiters were of various ethnicities: Filipino, Chinese, Hawaiian, Samoan.

After the light lunch I proceeded to the main lounge to my first staff meeting. Everyone was there, and the presentation was informal. Mr. Rudiger first introduced the ten musicians of the band and orchestra, then the dance team of instructors. They were a very nice couple, both slim and trim. Then on to the introduction of the hostess, a young woman of thirty, then the bridge and tournament teacher, and the performers, a young Filipino dancer and his Hawaiian wife. Mr. Rudiger introduced the speaker, who would give lectures of the various places that the ship would visit, and the staff of the American Express travel agency and the two escorts for the offshore tours. Next came the couple who tended the gift shop and finally I was introduced as the art and language instructor. The last of the introductions was of the interdenominational faith chaplain and his wife. We were all served cocktails and hors d'oeuvres. We mingled and got acquainted with one another. I learned that the dance instructors were from San Francisco and I got friendly with them. Soon we made plans together to go ashore in Japan. Our next port of call was Hawaii, still in the U.S. territory.

The next few days at sea consisted of inventorying the art materials. Mr. Rudiger told me that we would start classes after we left Honolulu, our first port where we were to acquire more passengers with several disembarking. The ship had a beauty salon and I knew that my friend Lottie Randall would be on that cruise as a beautician. We had known each other for many years and it was good to have a friend on the ship. Lottie and I went ashore in Honolulu, and I remember sipping cool mai-tais while we sat at the round bar on the beach of the Royal Hawaiian hotel. We watched the bathers and surfers until the afternoon darkened into evening. The flamboyant sunset on the horizon faded away until finally the torches on the beach had to be lit. We returned to the ship and that evening included a special Hawaiian dinner complete with entertainment by hula dancers. The women passengers wore colorful muumuus and the men, aloha shirts. The show ended just before we sailed. Beautiful hula dancers with grass skirts put fragrant leis of flowers around the necks of men. Everyone talked animatedly in the passageways. The bar was full, as were the lounges. Many passengers held cocktail parties in their cabins or staterooms. The siren sounded, the whistle blew, and the signal struck for "All ashore that's going ashore." Amidst confetti, streamers, and Hawaiian music playing on deck and on the pier, we sailed from Honolulu, past the Aloha Tower, to the open sea, to our next destination and my first glimpse of mysterious Japan and its port of Yokohama.

chapter Four

THE DAILY BULLETIN slipped under my cabin door proclaimed a boat drill was to be conducted in the morning. I was scheduled to have a registration for my classes at two in the afternoon. I planned for two groups of students: the first would be for advanced students, each with at least one art class to his or her credit; and the second group for students with no experience in art. I found that the card room, a small room used for informal card games, had been assigned to me! I went to Mr. Rudiger's office to get supplies to register passengers for my art and language classes. I arrived in the card room at two p.m. and some passengers stopped by to inquire about the art classes. Patiently I explained my program, that I would teach charcoal drawing of still life and watercolor composition and scenery. A few people signed up for my classes, but I had only another half hour of scheduled registration. On an average cruise of four hundred passengers, I should be able to get ten percent, I calculated. But I wasn't near that number. The average age of the "Round-the-World" passengers was seventy-five years young. When a small group of elderly ladies walked in, I smiled and tried to entice each of them to sign up. Two more couples came in the card room and a tall gray haired man asked if the classes would have any nude models. If so, he would like to join. That broke the ice and they all signed up. We chatted and joked. All told, I had twenty-four students on that first registration day for the art classes. I explained to the small group that the ship furnished all the materials and the works they produced under my guidance would be theirs to keep. I also explained that we would have an art exhibit of all the students' works at the end of the cruise to include a cocktail party with prizes and awards for the best works. That announcement excited all the registrants and they left in good spirits. I was elated and determined to make the classes fun and interesting and not to make too many serious criticisms.

At cocktail time passengers gathered in the bar. It was strange to see a few matronly women climbing on high bar stools. In any event all had a good time.

The next day my classes started. The ship rolled gently and I had put drawing papers on the table with long pieces of chalk. I had gone to the galley and asked for a bowl of assorted fruit to be brought to the class for our subject. A young man from the galley staff brought a fruit bowl. The first class was my beginners. About fifteen people sat at a long table in front of their drawing papers, awaiting my instructions. With a calm voice, just like I spoke to my child, I explained the various shapes and sizes and volume of the fruits in the bowl. I told my class to sketch what they saw in front of them. A few of the bolder students drew gigantic apples, bigger than the pineapple and grapefruits. Their bananas looked like wobbly snakes; the lemons, like eggs. I patiently went over to each student and demonstrated on the corner of the drawing paper how to balance the shapes and volume by comparing circles, squares, triangles. Soon my beginners started to get the idea. I saw a few good drawings emerge. The students then were instructed to step back from their papers and to look at their sketches from a distance and compare them with the actual subject. Mistakes could be easily corrected when viewed from a distance. After the hour had passed, I politely thanked everyone and all left the classroom. Some were a little frustrated, no doubt, but in general, everyone left seemingly encouraged by their first attempts. It was difficult for them to instantly achieve realistic effects because they had not worked with chalk and crayons since their early years.

A sour note occurred after class. I was summoned to the cruise director's office. As I went in, by the look on Mr. Rudiger's face, I knew I had done something wrong. He then told me rather rudely, never to go to the galley without orders and not to ask the crew for anything, without proper authorization written by a purser. I had not gone through proper channels. In the future I was to report directly to the purser's office and put my request to the attention of the chief steward. I felt humiliated and walked out of the office in tears. But I soon realized that it would be a long trip indeed if I let myself be bullied and be so sensitive about it.

By evening I was calm. I put on my best dress, a lavender chiffon that I had purchased at Neiman Marcus in Dallas. That dress still fit my size six figure. That evening was to be a formal cocktail party for the presentation of the ship's officers by Captain Virgil Hendryx. In the lounge, men in smart tuxedos and ladies in glamorous evening gowns were assembled. A dozen officers of the ship, smart-looking in their dark uniforms, stood in line to greet the world cruise passengers. Captain Hendryx was the first in line and each officer was presented by the hostess, who was also dressed in her evening finery. The captain was a charming man, about sixty with white hair and a ruddy complexion, rather stout with a chest full of decorations. Next to the captain, I saw a tall, blond-haired man in his forties with blue eyes and a crinkly smile. He was the first mate, second in command. As I shook hands with him, I noticed his soft, dry palm with a strong shake. Then I proceeded to be presented and greeted by all the rest of the officers from various departments including navigation, engineering, stewards, radio room, and the ship's doctor. After the presentations, everyone was sipping champagne and eating caviar. The enormous buffet was decorated with ice statues and the emblems of the President's line, featuring our ship, the *President Roosevelt*. As I stood by the buffet, the tall blond officer leaned over me to get a canapé of smoked salmon. I met his blue eyes and without shame said that I didn't recall his name. He told me that it was Sven Troyson and with a trace of an accent he told me he was Norwegian. We chatted about the trip and my function on the cruise. Soon we were seated at a crowded table in the bar talking to other passengers. To my left was a middle-aged couple from Florida, next to me was Sven and I could feel the warmth of his body. Kyle, the ship photographer, appeared and took several pictures of our group. I saw Sven's eyes wandering about, but returning to me often. The champagne made me animated and everyone found me cute and charming. I felt elated. I detailed the program of my art classes for the trip. There was a lot of laughter, noise, gaiety, and fun. The dinner was equally festive. I was assigned my own table with five lovely ladies. On most cruises the ratio was ten women to one man. When I came back to my cabin that evening I felt very good. I was attracted to Sven and he seemed attracted to me. I wondered about him a lot before going to sleep.

The next morning, we were to have a boat drill at ten o'clock. Everyone was to be on assigned decks facing a lifeboat. We had to wear our life jackets. We were to follow the orders given to us through the loudspeakers to learn how to act in case of an emergency. Each boat had a designated officer in command. As I was standing with the other passengers on deck, garbed in the Mae West life jacket that gave me a strange silhouette, I caught a glimpse of Sven on the navigation bridge above us, looking out over the drill. The photographer Kyle was ever-present with his camera, taking photos that later would be posted in his shop. The tiny shop displayed photographs of the ship's passengers busy at their various activities, and was a favorite stop after dinner for the passengers. Kyle's business was brisk and he worked late hours in his darkroom.

There was something to do every day at sea, from early morning to the midnight buffet. Every hour offered opportunities for bridge lessons, art classes, travel lectures, movies, bingo games, tea, bowling on deck, dance lessons, calisthenics, crafts, costume contests, hat contests, concerts, and many other activities. Passengers could also tour the engine room, visit the galley, or even the bridge. Cocktail parties were held every night and the passengers could dance until the wee hours.

On a cold, gray day we arrived in Yokohama. When the formalities were over, the passengers could disembark. The ship was to stay four days in port, so the passengers would have the opportunity and time to take tours to Kyoto, Nikko, or Nara to view the various temples and see the sights. The formalities would be the same in each port. All passengers assembled in the main lounge and a purser would come with passports to be stamped by the proper authorities of that country. There was a different procedure for the ship's staff. We had to join the crew in their quarters to get passes that would identify each of us. The passes would be valid for the time that the ship was in the foreign country's port. This was the first time I saw the crews' quarters. This area of the ship was very different from the passengers' wide corridors and elegantly appointed cabins. Here the hallways were narrow, cramped, all steel and iron. The cabins, through open doors, revealed four to six cots, some men in underwear and sandals wandered about. A mixture of Tagalog, Chinese, Samoan, Hawaiian was spoken among the cooks, waiters, galley helpers and deck hands. As we stood in line to get our passes, some crew members read newspapers, while others listened to small radios. I stood with the dance team, who were as eager as I was to go ashore. With the pass in my purse, I joined my friends to walk down the gangplank as a strong stench of fish and gasoline struck our nostrils. Many Japanese freighters and other ships were also in port. We had to walk half a mile to the gate that was guarded by two white-gloved Japanese policemen. We showed our passes and were allowed to go through the gate. We had been officially admitted to Japan.

We found a taxi and told the driver to take us to Motomachi, the center of town. Soon we arrived in a crowded district with banners blowing in the wind, banners that were covered with strange red and white characters. Everything seemed in reduced scale: lovely girls in kimonos, hair lacquered, geishas with obis, wooden shoes, people carrying small folded kerchiefs of cotton. Old ladies bent, young people with umbrellas, curious oval-eyed children, smiling like elves, with school books strapped to their backs. We wandered in and out of shops. In Japan everything had a proper place on immaculate shelves; it was very decorative. I was looking for art materials, small frames, brushes, ink. Strange, but harmonious, music poured from loudspeakers. I was enchanted and purchased several tapes. We sat in a tiny café and I had the best cup of coffee of my life. Then we went to the train station, where I noticed many Japanese were wearing white surgical masks. I was troubled by it, thinking they had a contagious disease. But I learned this custom was a courtesy to protect others from the masked people's cold germs.

Tokyo was overwhelming. We found the Ginza and walked at great length. Shops, department stores, gigantic signs in neon, tiny cafés, sushi bars. Then we stopped to eat yakitori. We were served a small portion of shrimp tempura, something gelatinous but not unpleasant. It was there that I learned about the ginkgo nut trees that lined the street. In a small alley we found an antique shop. I purchased a lovely imari plate, and also a small satsuma dish. I just fell in love with the objects of art, and I discovered in me the Collector. Although I didn't have much money, I spent all I had that day with no remorse. I was happy. We returned to the ship exhausted, I holding my treasures, my friends lugging their purchases on board.

We had three more days in Yokohama. The second day I went to the silk hotel then to Kamakura to view the Great Buddha. I purchased a string of amber-colored beads. I did some sketching while a curious group of Japanese businessmen watched me. I stopped to look at some scrolls stretched out on the sidewalk before returning to the ship. As I was doing so, Kyle snapped a photo of me.

Another day at sea and we arrived in Kobe. The weather was cold, the air crisp, the sky very blue. The port of Kobe was very clean. I had heard of Kobe steak and was curious to try it. When we entered the restaurant and ordered our meals, I tasted the most succulent, butter-tender piece of beef. It was easy to cut with a fork. I went to a train station where I learned I could go skiing for the day. An eager young Japanese offered to be my guide to Mount Rokko, a popular ski resort of the area. It was exhilarating. After days of looking at the ocean, I would see some snow. The Japanese were enthusiastic downhill skiers: young people, old folks, even children, all following one another down the slopes. The resort was surrounded by low mountains.

The next day I went to Kyoto with the tour. We admired the Temple of Sanjusangendo, with the whispering floors. We went to the Golden Pavilion, set on a lake so serene, with its golden reflection. I endeavored to paint it later and took lots of photos wherever I went. I was never without my camera, sketchpad, pens, and pencils. Later I acquired an 8-millimeter camera and made some movies.

The next day was a smooth day of sailing through the inland sea. The giant red Torri Gate emerged from the deep blue ocean. All the passengers were busy the next few days with classes, cocktail parties, and, of course, the hat parade. The art classes progressed smoothly and more passengers signed up after a few weeks at sea. In a few days we were to be in Hong Kong. I was elated when told that it was a shopper's paradise.

We docked in the Hong Kong terminal early one morning. After the formalities, I was one of the first on the ship to disembark, so eager was I to explore this exotic land. The terminal reminded me of a giant mall, stores everywhere, all lit up, very modern: cafés, restaurants, yet strangely everything seemed a little too clean and sterile. But once outside the terminal, Hong Kong was very different. Narrow streets with muddy roads; signs in Chinese, Cantonese, Mandarin, Hindi, English; people walking briskly; a jam of push-carts, rickshaws, and cars; Chinese and Europeans mingling. Hong Kong was under British rule then. Sailors and tourists strapped with cameras and shopping bags, all added to the din. Laundry hung from windows, young boys and girls carried trays of food balanced on bamboo poles across their shoulders. Here I was at last in the shoppers' mecca. I was looking at the card in my hand for the address of the tailor I wanted to see. Soon I found the tiny shop tucked in an alley. I walked in and inquired about Mr. Chan. Presently, an elderly Chinese gentleman came to greet me. I explained that I was from the ship and would like a copy of a suit that I had brought with me. After viewing his selection of beautiful materials, I settled on a lovely raw silk, with gold lining. I was offered a glass of strong tea and we began to discuss the price. After much talk, I was able to get the work done for half the original price, which was, I am sure, what they expected customers to pay in the first place. Chinese were very perceptive and they knew that human nature loves to bargain. And they also enjoyed the game.

My money was dwindling and we were only three weeks into the long voyage. I had to be conservative but I could see myself in that lovely cream-colored silk suit complete with gold lining for the evening galas on the ship, admittedly, to impress a certain officer. I was still intrigued with Sven, and at a cocktail party I danced with him. I was terribly excited but he didn't depart from his cool and formally polite manners. After the dance, he returned me to my table companions, several lovely elderly ladies, all students of my art classes. They had been watching me on the dance floor. One of them remarked that we made a lovely couple.

I came upon the Peninsula Hotel and its beautiful marble lobby with exquisite decorations. Young bellboys wearing small beige uniforms topped by pillbox hats and white gloves opened the big glass doors. A fleet of impressive Rolls Royces and Bentleys were parked in front near the two stone lions at the entrance. I went to the mezzanine to have a fuller view of the people having tea and lunch. The main floor was crowded with travelers, prosperous Chinese merchants entertaining clients, lovely, beautifully groomed Chinese girls with their escorts, tourists wearily sitting in the lobby with shopping bags at their feet. Occasionally a bellboy would cross the lobby while holding a blackboard with a name on it and would ring a chime. I visited the stores in the Peninsula Hotel, the wares all luxurious, especially expensive jewelry of diamonds, ruby, emerald, gold, all precious and semi-precious stones of the world.

I walked out dazzled and hungry so I stopped in a café by the President Hotel for a sandwich and coffee. I didn't want to waste precious shopping time. I hesitated between the Hong Kong side and Kowloon. I opted for the antique market near Cat Alley on a small, narrow and smelly street. It was, however, so picturesque that I did some quick drawings, while curious children in rags watched me. An old woman carried a large load of wood on her back, young women with babies strapped to their backs. A man squatted in front of some trinkets to sell and among them I detected some old jade pieces. I asked to see the pieces. They seemed genuine so I paid the price he asked, as it seemed a fair price and the pale light jade felt cool in my hand.

While at sea, Captain Hendryx was keenly interested in all shipboard activities and would pay us a visit to view my students' works. One evening at cocktail time, I overheard the captain and some passengers talking about a legendary lady called Old Hong Kong Mary. She was a hundred and three years old and lived in the New Territories. I was curious about her and told Captain Hendryx that it would be a privilege to meet the old lady. Her story intrigued me. As a young Chinese girl, having left her family in mainland China, she came to Hong Kong in the late eighteen hundreds and went to the docks as a washerwoman, taking in laundry of the merchants and seamen. She got married and had four sons. Her husband died. but she continued her work with the help of her sons. The captain remembered her coming to the ships to collect the sailors' dirty clothes. Soon she installed a small table by the docks and sold goods and trinkets or lent money at a substantial interest rate to the sailors and merchants. At the age of forty, she was buying real estate and she and her sons amassed a small fortune. In her old age, she owned a large part of Hong Kong: shops, hotels, land, and businesses that were managed by her sons. When young Princess Margaret of England visited Hong Kong, the one person she was interested in meeting was old Hong Kong Mary. Presently she was living with one son in a small village in the new Territories. The captain told me he would arrange for me to meet her, when I told him I would be honored to sketch the old lady.

The next morning, while in the port of Hong Kong, as I was standing in the foyer by the purser's office, I saw the captain and an elderly Chinese gentleman coming toward me. I was introduced to Mr. Ma, son of Hong Kong Mary. A car was waiting for us. Holding my camera and my sketchpad, I thanked the captain and off Mr. Ma and I went, through the sprawling busy cityscape and onto the countryside. It was so different from Kowloon or Hong Kong. I saw the countryside of China: green rice fields, farm houses, women with heads covered by large hats with black fringe working in the fields, more dry land, a small village, children, chickens, pigs. We drove on top of a hill to a large house in the middle of a bamboo field. Mr. Ma guided me to a porch and asked me to wait. A few minutes passed and a servant came out carrying a tiny old lady with practically no hair, and extremely small feet. The servant set her on a lovely antique rosewood chair and placed a plaid coverlet on her lap. After introductions, tea was served. She was told that I was an artist and a friend of the captain. She gave me a toothless smile of recognition. On my sketchpad, I worked a few fast strokes of charcoal. Mr. Ma was standing beside me and watching with interest. Suddenly, the old lady turned her head and with one finger pointed to her cheek. The translation was that, this was her best side. Her son also told me that next she pointed to the top of the hill and again the translation was that she wanted to be buried there, facing mainland China. The hour passed swiftly and I made a few good drawings. Later, I gave a drawing to the captain. We drove back to the ship. I had taken lots of photos also, and was glad to have met old Hong Kong Mary.

The next day I went to Aberdeen and saw the floating restaurants with hundreds of junks and saipans with their colorful sails. The harbor was so crowded that the many nimble Chinese were jumping from one junk to the next one, carrying pots and pans, sacks of flour, vegetables, and various goods. Entire families lived on those boats and clothes were hung on deck. Even small dogs lived on junks with their human families. I wondered if the

my first visit to
Hong Kong 1969

Chinese ate the dogs, as I had heard. I took the ferry from Kowloon to the Hong Kong side to Victoria Peak and rode the tram to enjoy the beautiful view. I stopped at the Mandarin Hotel, one of the most luxurious hotels in the world. But I was drawn to the waterfront, teeming with life. I found a crate where I could sit and sketch the small food stalls everywhere, people eating while squatting near boiling pots of strange concoctions. I took a rickshaw to ride the smelly narrow streets. I browsed in a dark antique store and made a small purchase. I walked the narrow alleys, so steep. Women squatted to sell fruit, in large round shaped containers that were carried on the end of bamboo poles balanced on the women's shoulders. There were Chinese signs everywhere and on every balcony clothes hanging. I took a small boat back to Kowloon. The old woman at the stern was wearing a large coolie hat. I bought it from her for a couple of dollars. She was delighted as it was probably worth a tenth of the price. I was happy with my acquisition. I wore the coolie hat to do my sketching as the weather turned hot. It was November 1968.

I returned to the ship that evening with many sketches, my hat, small purchases, and lots of finished rolls of film to be developed. Mail was put under my door in my cabin, letters from Lillian, from my son, and a couple of cards from Benny Bufano. On my first trip around the world I was to get many post cards and an occasional letter from Benny Bufano. I hastily replied to all and got some sleep. I eventually made five trips around the world from 1968 to 1972. Not all these voyages were the same, but I will return to that issue later.

The next day was our last in Hong Kong so I returned to Chan the tailor and got my raw silk suit, with the gold striped lining. As I was looking at a jewelry store, I noticed a lovely jade ring in the window. I went in on an impulse and bought it. It had a lovely green color, an oblong shape, and two gold nuggets on each side. I never had to regret that purchase and starting then, I fell in love with jade and have been collecting it ever since: small pieces, jewelry, bangles, and necklaces. I also went in the large emporium at the terminal where all of China was represented. There were huge porcelain vases intricately painted, Chinese rugs, a large variety of goods, carvings, ho tai, guan yen, Foo dogs of various sizes. Also many exotic masks from mysterious gods of the Orient, such as Quan Yen represented in porcelain, wood, ivory. A wealth of ivory objects was for sale in the large bazaar.

Even back in 1968 Hong Kong was overpopulated. At night the magnificent harbor of Hong Kong came alive with a multitude of neon lights, so bright it seemed like daylight in the streets. One of the best values was to ride the ferries back and forth from Hong Kong to Kowloon for twenty-nine cents. But everything was a great bargain. Women passengers would wait to get their hair done in the Hong Kong beauty salons for just four or five Hong Kong dollars. We sailed that evening for Singapore, a two-day cruise at sea. The time passed quickly. We had a crew party in Lottie's cabin that she shared with two other girls who worked as beauty salon operators. Everyone was talking about their purchases and their good time in Hong Kong. We had wine and hors d'oeuvres. Kyle stopped by also to show us the photos he had taken.

In Singapore, Malaysia, the weather was hot and muggy on deck. But everyone was there to watch the lion dance being performed by an energetic group of young dancers in richly decorated costumes. Malaysian drums kept the beat and the movements of the dark-skinned dancers were very rhythmic. My impression of Singapore was of a modern and clean city, with tall buildings and large, air-conditioned hotels on Orchard Road. The Malaysian Hotel, richly decorated with colorful batik paintings in the hotel lobby. The famous Raffles Hotel, a turn-of-the-century building, had large ceiling fans in the bar. In the surrounding gardens exotic palm trees, orchids, old rattan chairs and tables spoke of a bygone era, the times of Somerset Maugham. I visited Tiger Baum Garden, a park full of curiously grotesque statues. I paused and did some drawings at the gate and spoke to the turbaned, mustached gardener. The ship's tour was passing by at that moment and Kyle took some pictures of me on Orchard Road. I passed by the antique store called Moon Gate. I went in and bought a beautiful antique cloisonné incense burner, after much bargaining. It was exquisitely packaged in a silk box and my most ambitious purchase yet.

I walked to the Chinese part of the city, with its small artisan shops, filled with exotic carvings, brass, wood, ivory, jade. The exotic people: beautiful Malaysian women, a mixture of Chinese, Hindu, Filipino, Malay, black, Thai, and white, with Chinese features, golden skin, shining hair, friendly smiles. I joined a few members of the ship's crew and we ambled along the famous "Boogy" Street, where the spectacle was a continuous parade of the most beautiful, exotic girls in colorful and sexy costumes of various undress. It was part of the red light district. Café patrons could enjoy a drink while watching the parade of prostitutes, who were mostly young Malaysian boys.

The next day, I took a tour, a four-hour ride in the Malaysian countryside to the Jim Thompson plantation. The large house, made of the most beautiful teak wood, was surrounded by banana palms and exotic shrubbery. We were greeted by a staff of young turbaned boys who showed us the house with its

monks in saffron
robes by the
temples in
Bangkok.

beautiful teak furniture, oriental carvings, statues, and silk pillows of all colors and shapes. At a small shop could be purchased raw silks by the yard. Our group was treated to a buffet, set in the outdoor garden. I sampled satay, a dish of skewered beef in peanut cream. We danced after dinner. Jim Thompson was not there and it would be some ten or fifteen years later that we learned of his disappearance and mysterious death.

We returned to the ship that was sailing the next day for Bangkok, Thailand, city of a thousand temples and canals. On a hot and humid day I got off the gangplank and walked in the city teeming with people, monks in saffron robes, pushcarts, and rickshaws. I took all in that morning and returned to the coolness of the ship at lunchtime. In the afternoon I took a tour with other passengers to view the Temple of the Jade Buddha. I particularly admired the gold carvings outside the temple, or the palace, as the locals called it. Fascinating sculptures, half gods, half birds. The large stone figures guarding the doors with their swords, the sloping roofs shaped like a pagoda, the graceful dog figures, gold leaf everywhere. It was intricately and richly carved and yet it had grace and simplicity. We were then whisked to a boat on the klongs, the water a dark green emerald color. I had my camera ready, the luxuriant vegetation on the banks of the klong, houses built on stilts or simply shacks on the banks of the canals. Women hanging clothes, men smoking pipes. A boat was loaded with rich, ripe fruits and vegetables, green watermelons, bananas. Another boat was fragrant with exotic flowers, orchids in pastel colors. We saw a lovely Thai girl with almond eyes, shiny hair, dark golden skin, who looked at us and smiled. The boat stopped at the Oriental Hotel dock and we stepped into one of the most beautiful hotels in the world, with its cool marble lobby, colorful sarong clad girls guiding our group to tables set outside facing a stage. Drinks were set and we made ourselves comfortable. We were treated to a graceful ballet of exquisite Thai dances. The young dancers dressed in gold tiaras, shimmering gold and purple sarongs, slow motion hands like birds and long-nailed fingertips pointed heavenward. The melodious music was enchanting. Two dancers came and staged a mock duel dance, wearing grimacing masks. After the show, we toured the hotel, marveling at the pool, the bar, restaurants and even the bathrooms. Then back on the boat to continue our visit of the canals, more temples with steep stairs, more carvings, spirit houses, then to an area of small shops and souvenir displays. I bought a gilded Buddha figurine and a wooden pedestal. Bangkok was a good place to buy gems and precious stones, rubies, sapphires. But our next port was to be Ceylon and I was told the stones were less expensive.

Some of the passengers had taken another tour, a two-day journey to Chang Mai, to see the forest and the place where elephants bathed. We also made a stop at Pattaya Beach, a resort with hotels.

That evening, drinking cocktails on board the ship, women wore their silk dresses and blouses from Hong Kong, and displayed their jewelry. My art students showed me their purchases and I admired their lovely silk gowns. The atmosphere was joyous and festive and everyone was talking about a show that was scheduled on board. The passengers were to be the performers and I was the coordinator for costumes and make-up. The revue was a mixture of Broadway songs and vaudeville acts. The rehearsal went well, the drinks free and plentiful, all supervised by the cruise director. By curtain call, the cast had imbibed much liquor and on the stage the results were hilarious. All had a great time, audience and actors. After the show, I saw Sven, dancing in his white uniform with Elsie Dukas, a wealthy woman passenger. She was a lively sixty-year-old redhead, determined to have the time of her life. She was very popular and I suspected her to be having an affair with the ship's doctor. I had seen them cozy one night, very late in the bar, as I came upon them after my walk on deck. The weather was so balmy, the night so peaceful, millions of stars visible in the skies, the dark water below, ship sailing smoothly, a nostalgic feeling overcame me.

The next morning, we arrived in Colombo, Ceylon (later it became Sri Lanka). I came ashore clad in a summer dress; for coolness my long hair was parted in the middle and tied with a rubber band around each ear. Colombo had high heat and was very humid. It was even hotter than Bangkok. As a small group of local dancers was performing on the deck, I spotted Lottie and Kyle. We all climbed into a rickety bus that was going to Mont Lavinia, some sixty miles away on the coast. We came upon the Mont Lavinia Hotel, a relic from the past, but the beach was lovely with small, dark-skinned women dressed in colorful saris selling shell necklaces. Their figures were like Tanagra statues, small with supple waists, like dancers. Lottie and I bought cowry shell necklaces and walked back to the hotel, passing small jewelry and gem shops. I bought a blue sapphire princess ring and Lottie also made a purchase.

The second day, I was asked to be an escort for a tour going to Kandy, a village high in the mountains, some six hours by train. About twenty-five passengers and the tour director were gathered at the station. For the day's journey we had a clean compartment on the train, which was chartered by American Express Tours. My companions were two lady passengers and

Kyle. As we began to climb, an incredible spectacle unfolded before our eyes: miles and miles of lush green fields. Women collected tea leaves in big baskets tied to their backs. They wore saris of the most vivid colors, pink, yellow, red, gold. They were like flowers in the green, lush fields, their dark skin shining, their clothes from deep purple to fuchsia to mauve, pink, orange. I wanted to paint what I saw, but was only able to take photographs and do some sketching. However, my memories retained that spectacle forever and later I did a beautiful oil painting of that scene.

We had excellent service on the train, young women in saris would come in the steaming compartment with silver trays of sliced cool pineapple to refresh us. In Kandy, a bus was waiting for us and we were brought to the Kandyan Temple of the Tooth. The legend was that a real tooth of Buddha was enshrined in the Temple and once a year with much pageantry, it was paraded in the streets of Kandy in a procession of richly decorated elephants wearing brocade, precious stones, and palanquins. The relic was in a gold casket. People wore their best, elaborate and richly decorated costumes. The Kandyan band and dancers escorted the procession. The elephants were treated like royalty. Their ornaments were the richest imaginable with gold, rubies, emeralds, sapphires. The elephants' tusks were covered with carved silver ornate with rubies. I had hoped to see the spectacle, but we came at the wrong time of year. However, those images stayed in my mind for a lifetime. Next, we went to see the elephants bathe in a water hole. Small dark elephants were being scrubbed by the native boys. As a small elephant was crouching, a boy asked me in gestures, if I wanted to ride on it. I acquiesced and with his help, I was on top of the elephant. It was a strange sensation. I was half exuberant, half scared, and held tightly to some strong elephant hairs. Kyle quickly snapped a few pictures, which became my souvenirs of Ceylon.

In the evening on board the ship, I took a last look at Colombo as we sailed from the Indian Ocean to Bombay. The next day, the ship docked at Bombay. The ship stayed there five days, our longest time ashore, to facilitate the American Express train tour on its visit to Agra and the Taj Mahal. I was able to work my way onto the tour as an escort. The next morning forty-five passengers climbed aboard the special chartered train; this included the cruise director, the photographer, and me. After breakfast that first morning, I joined a small party and we went to the Taj Mahal Hotel on the waterfront with a lovely view of the Gates. A small tour had gone to see the Elephanta Caves while Kyle and I walked on the waterfront. We took a taxi, driven by Kala Sing, a smiling Sikh. We asked him to give us an hour tour of the city. After we agreed on the number of rupees, he first took us to see the Gandhi shrine with the silver statue of Mahatma Gandhi, then to see Gandhi's spartan room, where he lived an ascetic life. Next we went to Crawford Market, Bombay's largest, a pungent place where I was fascinated by the spices. Displayed in large sacks on the floor were fragrant cardamom, cumin, curries of all varieties; also displays of fruits, vegetables, flowers on straw mats. Hindu men sat cross-legged in front of brass bowls. White-mustached, turbaned old men, Sikhs with their red turbans. Bombay was a busy, bustling metropolis. Children had large, dark eyes and distended bellies. Many beggars squatted everywhere, some without limbs. Also young Hindu girls with dark eyes and shiny black hair, white teeth showing in smiles. The streets were crowded with all sorts of vehicles and animals. Cows would often walk in the middle of the streets and people would let them pass as cows were considered sacred and believed to be reincarnated. Bombay was a city in constant motion.

We visited a Jain Temple, where worshipers were neither Buddhist nor Hindu. The Hindu religion believes in cremating the dead so the soul can be free to be reincarnated. Jainism was founded by a Hindu reformer in the sixth century as a revolt against the caste system. We went to see Bombay's mosque and our driver came upon a street lined with cages. He explained that women, young and old, as well as children, lived in those cages to survive and were prostitutes for food. It was a sad place. Then our driver left us at the docks to return to our ship. We tipped him generously and took many pictures with him.

After a good night's sleep, we were ready to take our train journey to Agra to see the Taj Mahal. My feelings were ecstatic. I was living a dream and as I packed a small bag in my cabin, I was thinking how lucky I was to be on this trip. I had found friends, I was praised for my good work on the ship, my relations with the cruise director had improved, and I was gaining confidence and artistic practice. The morning of our departure arrived. The waiting bus at the pier took our group to the Bombay train station. A dismal sight awaited us; many people slept in the station on the quai and even on the rails. Our train compartment was clean; I was sharing it with Kyle. We had become very good friends, although I suspected he wanted to be more than that. The compartment had two beds and a toilet with a shower. As everyone got settled, the train departed. Our first stop was to be New Delhi. On leaving Bombay, the scenery was monotonous, dry land for miles on. After a light meal I took a shower. Kyle took a photo of me draped only in a towel. Then I went to sleep to the soft purring rhythm of the train.

The next morning a boy brought us some tea, and out the train window we saw a procession of people dressed in white: men, women, and children, all carrying brass containers on their heads. The scene reminded me of biblical times. We saw villages, shacks, a few trees, cows, water wells, farmers, and oxen plowing some dry fields. At a small station, the train stopped to pick up some fruit for our journey. While we waited, a small band of turbaned Hindus with white hair and mustaches, wearing old British military uniforms, performed military marches to music they played on their brass instruments. It was a touching sight as they looked so dignified.

The food on the train was exceptionally good. We were told not to drink tap water, but there was plenty of excellent hot tea and Coca Cola that I drank with no ice. The dining room car was immaculate, white damask tablecloths, polished silver, large overhead ceiling fans, efficient and polite Hindu waiters in their white uniforms and white caps on their heads. I liked the various Hindu foods, such as the curried lamb and varieties of rice.

Early in the afternoon we arrived in New Delhi. Kyle and I took a taxi tour of the city. We made a stop at the New Oberoi Hotel, a beautiful modern hotel, marble lobby, fountain, elegant lounge and bar with Hindu motifs. New Delhi was rather modern, with many gardens and a university. The place had retained much of the British flavor of the past. The train was our hotel; we traveled mostly by night.

The next morning, we arrived in Jaipur, the pink city of the Maharajas. A car was waiting to take us to see the "Palace of the Wind" in the center of town. The building was soft pink, intricately carved like lace with little pagodas on each window. A legend told that when the wind blew, strange music filled the empty palace. Our car next drove through the crowded streets of Jaipur. I never saw so many camels, elephants, peaceful cows in the middle of a city. It was so strange with the exotic clothes, the turbaned men, the lovely women with their light saris. On the road to the Amber Palace, we stopped to see a snake charmer. My camera was never very far away and Kyle was always busy snapping pictures. Walking peacefully amidst cars and old trucks full of people were the cows. Nearby women were washing laundry.

The Amber Palace was surrounded by a fortress and all around the walls were a dozen elephants lined up waiting for our tour. They were to carry us to the top, to the entrance of the palace. Kyle and I rejoined the rest of our tour group to receive our elephant assignment. We climbed on the small seat attached to the elephant's back and we proceeded with the slow climb to the top. I felt I was on top of a moving mountain. As we swayed to and fro, the

Indian women
at the Taj Mahal

view was beautiful, as high as the roof of a one-story building. The experience was gratifying and we took many photos of the ascent. The old palace, one of the many left from the days of the maharajas, was beautiful. Artists and artisans were engaged in intricate restoration as the old palace was in need of repair. We visited the bar and lounge, very British colonial, with polo mallets on the walls, beautiful wood, rattan furniture. We had a stunning view of graceful columns with Hindu carvings. We were shown to the dining room, where we sat to lunch on delicious food to the accompaniment of Hindu music. After lunch, Kyle and I walked down to the center of town. We stopped at various bazaars. I bought a small ivory elephant, some loose, rough ruby stones, and a red Hindu tunic with leggings.

We returned to the train for the journey to Agra and the Taj Mahal. After a night's rest on the train, many cars were waiting to take the passengers to the Taj Mahal, as we arrived at a small station. Our little caravan made its way first to the ancient city of Fathepur Sikri, the capital in the old days, now a ghost town. It was nicely preserved but empty. The red flagstone terrace, the lush gardens in ruins surrounded the buildings of the same red stone as in Jaipur. A young boy of about ten followed Kyle and me as we were snapping pictures. We gave him some rupees and he flashed a toothy smile at us and gave us a hand salute. We took his picture for our memory albums.

We arrived at the Taj Mahal, one of the seven wonders of the world. For this momentous occasion, I wore dark red silk leggings and a red and gold tunic top, in the Hindu style, that I had purchased at the Emporium Bazaar. I also painted a red dot on my forehead and to complete the costume, I had a transparent silk scarf to put over my head. I wanted to blend into the scenery at this special place. The Taj Mahal was built between 1631 and 1653 by Emperor Shah Jahan as a monument for his wife Arjumand. Born in 1592, she was the daughter of Asaf Khan and married Shah Jahan in 1612. She died in 1631 after the birth of their fourteenth child. After the emperor's death, he was buried by her side. This was written on a marble plaque. Before entering the tomb, to fully appreciate the view of the Taj Mahal, one has to see it at four different times of day and night. At sunrise, it seems to float peacefully above the ground with its graceful columns standing like eternal sentinels and the soft cupola gleaming in the first rays of the sun. At midday, when the worshippers arrive, throngs of sari-clad women walk past the long pool, their colorful reflections in the water. In the early evening the Taj Mahal presents another vision of soft pink glistening marble. And in the moonlight it's a view of unsurpassed beauty, white minarets and cupolas and blue velvety starry skies. Someday I shall paint the beauty of the Taj Mahal again. It will live in my memory forever.

We boarded our train for the trip back to Bombay to rejoin our ship, the President Roosevelt. We had been at sea for six weeks, half our voyage. It would be nine long days at sea before we would see the coast of Africa, with Dakar our first port. We were sailing across the Indian Ocean, the weather was terribly hot and humid, but inside the ship it was cool and we resumed our ship's activities.

My art classes progressed rapidly, working on still lifes in watercolor. The French language classes held much interest as our next port was in Senegal and Dakar was a French-speaking country. All activities, including bridge tournaments, dance classes, lectures, bingo, and art, went well. The journal stated that there would be a meeting in the director's office that morning. While waiting for Mr. Rudiger to arrive, we were served coffee and pastries. We were briefed to what was called "the Arabian Night Pageant," a function that happened once a year on the world cruise. In a few days this very special event was to occur. Everyone was to wear their finest Oriental costumes and jewelry, including the crew members. A lavish dinner would be served on deck after a big cocktail party with music. A spectacular surprise show would follow. In the discussion of this show, Mr. Rudiger placed a box on his desk. Upon opening it, he showed us a pair of petite, transparent harem pants and a bolero of the same sequined material. He brought out a brassiere in aqua silk, an assortment of bells and bangles, a veil, and a gold coin belt. The task of belly dancing was assigned to me as my petite size would look quite fetching in that costume. I was to hide in a giant papier mâché mock cake, shaped like Aladdin's lamp, and pop out of the opening in the top at the designated time while holding a magnum of champagne. I was to walk slowly and provocatively in my dancer's costume to the Captain's table and present him with the champagne. Next, I was to do a belly dance to the sound of the "Persian Market" tune played by the ship's band on deck. The band members would be costumed like Aladdin, complete with gold turbans. This program was to be a surprise to the passengers as I came out of the cake. I decided that I would enjoy myself and show my talent as a dancer as well.

The evening arrived. A large space was cleared in the middle of the ship on deck, with tables arranged as a large horseshoe shape and set with white tablecloths and flowers. In one corner, a bar was set up for the cocktail party. The night was balmy and the skies covered with millions of stars. Their constellations contributed to our magical Arabian night. The passengers arrived from their cabins, dressed in all their finest Oriental costumes and jewelry. The waiters standing at attention were dressed in white djellabah and fezzes. The maître d' wore a spectacular maharajah costume. Only the ship's officers wore their white regulation uniforms.

The cocktail party was going smoothly. I slipped out to go to my cabin to put on my Arabian Nights costume for the show. Lottie was on hand to arrange my hair and help with my make up. In the galley, Mr. Rudiger and the maître d' helped me to get into the Aladdin lamp-shaped cake. I was to push the top open after three knocks and come out of the cake. Four black, bare-chested "Nubian slaves" carried the cake, box, and me to the top deck. The orchestra played "The Persian Market" as the cake was placed in the center of the deck. Mr. Rudiger, after a speech, which I couldn't hear, got much applause. He knocked three times. I pushed the top and came out gracefully, holding the bottle of champagne, eliciting another round of applause. I spotted Kyle taking pictures frenetically. I walked to the captain's table, deposited the bottle, and started to dance slowly, moving my belly rhythmically to the sound of the orchestra. The passengers applauded again loudly.

The dinner was sumptuous. The junior officers had big eyes for me as I sat at the chief steward's table. Next, the photo session started. I was to pose with the maître d' Maharajah for photos and also with passengers. Then came pictures with the turbaned captain and the boys of the American Express tour. I saw Sven standing by himself and, getting bold as it was my special evening, I asked Kyle to take photos of both of us. Kyle complied. Sven smiled, a glint of desire in his eyes as he detailed my flimsy costume. The festivities went on late into the night on deck, with music, food, dancing. Business would be brisk at the photo shop the next morning, as Kyle had a frantically busy evening.

Mother Lola as a
young woman in Poland

Brother Dédé, Nadine, Mother, and Brother Albert,
in Paris during WWII

Malmaison children

Arriving in New York

Andy before entering Naval
Academy visiting New York

Maurice Chevalier and Nadine in Dallas
Cipango Club

Hollywood, 1956

Miami Beach, 1956

Painting in Mexico, 1957

A modeling job

Working at the Interlude Club, San Francisco, 1965

Official photo for the
American President Line, 1968

Gregg, age 3

Sketching patrons at various clubs in San Francisco

Taj Mahal - first voyage, 1968

Sketching in Ceylon - first voyage

On safari - our car broke down

Kala Singh, our guide in Bombay, India, near Gandhi shrine

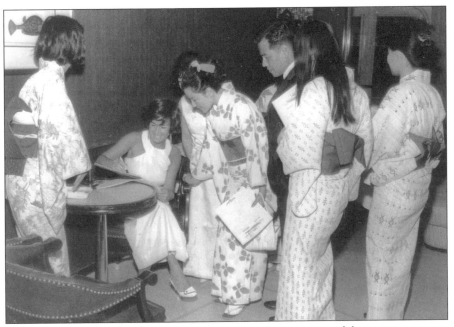

Sketching aboard ship - Japanese girls

In Bali with Temple dancers

Atop an elephant in Ceylon near Kandhy

Paris, first visit after 10 years in United States

Sketching "Cat Alley," Hong Kong

Visiting artists in Ubud, Bali

Cesaria, Israel - visiting friends from "Malmaison," 1982

Painting Provence - St Paul de Vence

Frank Sinatra at Nadine's art exhibit,
Monte Carlo, Monaco, 1987

Hotel de Paris - Monte Carlo, Nadine's art exhibit, 1986

H.S.H. Prince Albert of Monaco accepting a painting with
Nadine in the Grimaldi Palace, Monaco, 1986

Sketching the "Faraglione," Capri, Italy

Nadine teaching an art class aboard ship, 1968

Nadine's art exhibit aboard ship

SS *President Roosevelt* in Port of Samoa, 1968

Benny Bufano and Nadine, 1969

Chapter Five

W E HAD FOUR MORE DAYS at sea before sighting the coast of Africa. The ship anchored at Port Victoria, four days out of Bombay, in the Seychelle Islands with their lovely sandy beaches. I remember the giant turtles and all the turtle shell souvenirs at the dock. Upon returning to the ship I was called to Mr. Rudiger's office. He complimented me on my work with the passengers. He had sent a memo to the ship's company, American President Lines, in San Francisco, saying that "I was a bonanza" to the trip. He said that the office had put me on salary from then on, and asked me to join the ship on the next voyage around the world as an art and language instructor, in January, 1969. I was to get only five days between cruises. My thoughts went to my son whom I would only see for five days. But, to be honest, I was also overjoyed. I had performed my duties well. The passengers liked me, I was seeing the world in style and, now, if only I would have a chance at romance with Sven, everything would be perfect. For the past seven weeks, I had been returning alone to my cabin each night and I longed to be in a man's arms. Kyle did make some attempts to get close, but I was infatuated with Sven.

We arrived in Dakar in suffocating heat with a light, hot wind blowing on deck. I dressed lightly, took my camera and went ashore. The docks were crowded with merchants selling woodcarvings, black ebony elephants, gazelles, tigers, and lions. I walked by many stalls and observed the tall dark-skinned men wearing khakis, gesticulating and speaking French to the passengers. Beyond the docks was the marketplace. I saw dark-skinned women, carrying children on their backs, wearing colorful turbans and pareos. A watermelon vendor standing by the door was watching a lovely young turbaned girl go by. I quickly snapped a picture of the fleeting moment. Later I painted a picture from the snapshot I had taken. Walking on the waterfront I could see the Island of Ngoré. Returning to the docks, I ran into one of my art

Postcard 1 (front, illustrated):

KWUZAT HEFZIBAH – MOSAIC FLOOR
OF THE ANCIENT BETH ALPHA SYNAGOGUE
LE CARREAU DE L'ANCIEN SYNAGOGUE
DE BEIT-ALPHA

JOHN F. KENNEDY

my dear Nadine
this card will reach
you in Durban South
Africa — to day is
Jan. 30 so this will
get to y in time —
drop me a line from
There — may The
spirit of Peace bless
you —

Miss Nadine
Cruise Staff
S.S. President Roosevelt
Durban
John T. Rennie – Sons
P.O. Box 1006
Durban, Natal,
South Africa

THE ARK OF THE LAW WITH CEREMONIAL IMPLEMENTS   MADE IN ISRAEL
L'ARCH   6420

AIR MAIL

Postcard 2 (front, illustrated):

FS-587
MOJAVE YUCCA OR SPANISH BAYONET
(Yucca mohavensis)
The blooms of the Spanish Bayonet write spring
in large letters across the deserts of the west.
This plant is a short stemmed Yucca with a
beautiful blossom very similar to that of the
Joshua Tree. The two often grow in the same
general area.
Photo by Josef Muench

PLACE
STAMP
HERE

POST CARD

mia carissima Nadine
thank you for your
card and I pray that
you in good spirits
and happy this note
will be waiting for
you in Cristobel so
be it — god bless you
Beniamino —

miss Nadine
Cruise Staff S.S.
President Roosevelt
c/o Panama agencies
P.O. Box 1077
Cristobal, C.Z.

POST CARD

Postcard 3 (front, illustrated):

POST CARD

ADDRESS

my dear Nadine
this card will be
waiting for you
in Dakar and I
hope that you will
recieve a happy
wish on recieving
it — as you well
know I am hard at
work on my project
Love Beniamino

mis Nadine
Cruise Staff
S.S. President Roo...

for Jappan

© S.P.A.D.E.M., Paris & The Medici Society Ltd.,
London. Art Publishers by Appointment to the late
King George V. Engraved and Printed in Great Britain

106

students, Mrs. Lois Nielsen. She had always included me in her cocktail parties. We chatted and I kept her company while we walked toward a small shop. She saw me looking at some gold bangles and a carving of a Senegalese head of a woman. She bought both of them and gave them to me. I thanked her for her generosity. A few of the art student passengers had given me small gifts as tokens of their appreciation for my teaching and encouragement to them.

We returned to the ship, and after two more days at sea, we reached Durban, a modern city with large waterfront hotels. Tall Masai men, stationed by the hotels, stood ready to push their fares in bedecked rickshaws. The beach was crowded with bathers. I took refuge from the insufferable heat in the cool lounge of an old-fashioned hotel. In the evening, Kyle and I went to the Beverly Hotel in another part of the city.

Another night at sea and we arrived in Mombassa. I received mail that was put under my cabin door, letters from Lillian, from my little Gregg, and postcards from Benny Bufano. Everything was fine at home and they had received my mail. The next day, a safari was on the schedule. I was asked to be an escort on the tour to Tsavos Park, an all-day excursion. I had a day to myself in Mombassa for some shopping and taking of photos.

I walked off the ship on the gangplank to see the port of Mombassa. A huge pair of elephant tusks graced the entrance of the port. Like Durban, Mombassa had a large marketplace, crowded with woodcarvers. With displays of their sculpted animals at their feet, they carved with small sharp knives, then stained the wooden creatures to give texture in imitation of the natural skins and colorations of the animals. I stepped into a small shop filled with skins of tigers and gazelles, and elephants' feet. I bought an elephant hair bracelet and a tiger claw set in gold for a pendant to wear around my neck. Tusks of all kinds and ivory objects also were available. In 1968 it was not forbidden to import ivory. Elephants were not yet considered an endangered species.

I wandered the dusty city, snapping pictures in the indigenous quarters. I spotted two women wearing black purdahs and took a photo as they walked toward me. The younger covered her face. As they approached, I was suddenly surrounded by a dozen furiously vociferous, dark-skinned women, holding my arm, trying to get my camera. As I tried to disengage myself, I saw from the corner of my eye, a brokendown taxi driving by with four of the ship's crew. I yelled for help. They drove next to me and one of the men took my other arm and pulled me inside. He flung some coins and the women scur-

african Safari
Tsavos park. Kenya

ried to pick up the coins. I was to learn that the black-robed women belonged to a Khartoum Sudanese sect. They believed that in taking their picture, you stole their soul, or spirit. I was lucky that they didn't break my arm. We returned to the ship, my film intact and me still shaking.

The next day, a dozen small four-passenger vans were lined up on the docks waiting for a tour. It was our safari caravan. After the passengers boarded the vans, Kyle and I were assigned to the last one. It had an open roof in order to take pictures. We were assigned a chauffeur and a female guide, both were Masai. Early in the morning the caravan departed from the docks of Mombassa. I was wearing a khaki safari jacket of light cotton material, khaki shorts and a pith helmet. I had purchased my outfit the previous day in a shop in Mombassa. My ever-present camera and a sketchbook with charcoals were safely tucked in my over-the-shoulder bag. We drove for a few hours to Tsavos Park, to view the animals in their natural habitat. The scenery was ever changing as we drove: the crimson earth, strangely shaped trees, herds of gazelles on the flat horizon. We stopped at a promontory to view giraffes feeding on tree branches. We saw a couple of black rhinos looking very tame. The sky overhead was blue, in stark contrast to the red clay earth. Looming tall, huge elephants covered with the red clay dust, stood with their ears spread wide in the middle of the road, an all-together frightening sight towering above our vehicles. Buffalos, gazelles, ibis, all lived in harmony. We stopped for tea at Kilindini Lodge. Kyle was taking pictures left and right. Suddenly, there was a downpour, but it was short-lived. We kept driving, gazing at animals, and at each sighting, our Masai driver turned to us and smiled, showing his teeth filed to sharp points. Trying to read each other's minds, Kyle and I looked at each other.

Following our caravan, we kept on driving. The rain had ceased, and the air was still hot and humid. As I was putting another roll of film in my camera, the car stopped with a jerk. We heard a strange noise, and everyone got out. Our guide, after talking to the driver, explained to us that the car broke down, but not to worry as it would be repaired shortly. In the meantime, Kyle was taking pictures of the broken van. I remained seated in the van as I was afraid of snakes. No one had seen us stop and the last car had long vanished. After four long hours the car was finally fixed so we took our departure with our driver zigzagging through the bushes trying to find the caravan tracks. But they were not to be seen, having been washed out by the rain. We were lost and dusk was setting in. I was scared, but Kyle made jokes. A large red elephant loomed in front of us in the middle of the road. The guide explained to us that we must be still as elephants sometimes overturn cars. By now I was slightly panicking and even Kyle was nervous. After what seemed a long time, the driver found the tracks to the main road. We arrived at Kilindini Lodge, shaken but safe. No one in our caravan had yet arranged a search party. Everyone was happy to see us.

After a strong, hot tea, Kyle and I walked around the lodge to view the buffalo, antelopes, zebras, and gazelles drinking at the water hole. Driving back we stopped to view the blue monkeys in a dense forest area. At the dock, I shook hands with the Masai driver and our guide, happy to be back safely on board the ship.

Our next port was Cape Town, South Africa, a very lovely resort place, very European in feeling even though apartheid was still the custom in 1968. Lottie, Kyle, and I went to the beach to sunbathe. We met some young attractive Afrikaners and took some pictures. Later Lottie and I went shopping on Main Street. From every vantage point one could see Table Mountain, a large flat rock dominating the landscape. We went to Umschlanka Rock, to the beautiful very modern Hotel Beverly Hills. Cape Town had modern apartments and beautiful homes with well-tended gardens. South Africa produced an excellent wine, that we sampled. Geographically, we were in the southernmost tip of Africa. We saw two oceans meet.

Our next destination was Rio de Janeiro, Brazil. A cocktail party was held in the main lounge and I had a brief conversation with Sven. He was relaxed as the voyage was going well and commented that we had passed our halfway point in the voyage without major incident. He had heard of the success of my art classes and manifested a more serious interest in me. When he invited me to his quarters for cocktails the next evening, I was very happy and excited. Sven explained that it would have to be after 10 P.M. as any earlier a single person would attract attention. He explained that an officer could entertain a few passengers for cocktails. I was very flattered and anxious. We were to meet at 11 on the upper deck near Life Boat No. 10, just below the officers' quarters. I was wearing a chiffon dress of pale aqua with an embroidered bodice, and was very tan from the African sun. Sven arrived promptly, tall, slim in his white uniform with gold braid insignia on the shoulders. His blue eyes smiled at me. For a while, we didn't speak, we just stood by the railing, looking at the dark ocean below, listening to the sounds of waves, as a light breeze blew. Sven smoked a cigarette, I shivered slightly. He put his arm around me. We touched hands. I wanted to kiss him desperately but he held me tightly and looked at the horizon. After a while, we talked. We spoke of the trip, the passengers, the next port. Then he took my hand and escorted me to a stairway which led down to his quarters. With my stiletto heels I tried to climb the stairways. This was a passenger restricted area. We came to a plain metal door marked "Chief Mate" and I entered Sven's quarters, a large spacious cabin, with an extra large bunk bed, a desk, a shower, a toilet, very sparse and functional. In one corner, on a shelf, was an array of liquor bottles and glasses, also various plates with nuts, olives, and chips. There was a large comfortable leather chair near the desk, and a small armchair on which I sat. He fixed the drinks, a light bourbon and water for me and a scotch and soda for himself. We made some more small talk about the passengers and about my work. As we talked, Sven's voice took on an intimate inflection. His free hand dangled by the chair. I admired his neat fingernails and long tapered fingers. He took hold of my hand and gently pulled me to him. I found myself sitting on his lap, with one of his hands around my waist, the other still holding his glass of scotch. Sven pulled me closer to him and gently kissed my lips. At first, I did not know how to react, a little intimidated by the situation of being in an officer's quarters. But I returned his kiss with passion and he responded quickly by putting down his glass, standing up, and holding me very tightly. Gently he put me on the bunk. After that, all became a blur. We made passionate love, exploring each other's body, kissing every part. Everything was fast but infinitely tender. Later, when I began to dress, he said endearing words to me. We were whispering like conspirators. He indicated the way for me to go back to my cabin. It was 3 A.M. and all was quiet. Except for the officer on duty everyone was asleep on the ship. Sven said that he would call me later in the day. After a last kiss, holding my shoes in my hands, I left Sven's cabin, elated and happy. My adrenaline was pumping high in anticipation of possibly running into someone. But everything went smoothly and after a quick shower I snuggled into my pillow and went to sleep with wonderful dreams. So behind the cool facade, Sven did have a more intimate and passionate side. All the cells of my body were aching with the pleasure of love. I had wanted to sleep in Sven's arms but realized that it was impossible for the time being.

Later that day, I caught a glimpse of Sven on the bridge. As I climbed the forbidden stairs, he was there, but he merely glanced in my direction and gave me a stern look. I quickly retreated to the lounge. Had I upset him? Was I too bold? Too aggressive? Toward evening he called and asked me again to his quarters for drinks. I was overjoyed. We made wonderful, exciting love. After a few minutes' rest, he was able to have another erection and we had sex again

Rio de Janeiro Brazil
where I had my first "chagrin d'amour"

and climaxed together. His skin was hot and he had an odor of tobacco and aftershave. Afterwards in a tender moment we talked and sipped our drinks. We would be arriving in Rio de Janeiro in two days and Sven knew the city well. He said he would take me to dinner that first night in port.

Back in my cabin, I stared through the porthole and fantasized I was living a movie, a very romantic movie. My mind was already in Rio, a place I had never been but often dreamt of. I knew just what dress to wear for my first time in Rio: the tight-fitting, white chiffon. The same one I had worn on my honeymoon with Miles on the ship Matsonia. It was my mascot dress, very sexy.

The next two days, I worked very diligently at my classes. We were preparing our first passengers' art exhibit on board and all the students were involved. The watercolors would be framed and displayed on easels and presented at a cocktail party in the main lounge. The exhibit was to be held after our departure from Rio. My class consisted of thirty students and each one would exhibit two works, so the exhibit would have sixty watercolors, which would be judged on merit. All the non-artist passengers were invited to judge for the best in color, composition, subject, effort, and harmony. More than half of the artists would be awarded ribbons. The idea was to make everyone happy. Prior to departure from San Francisco, ribbons had been purchased, judging sheets printed; invitations typeset. The chief purser had asked the captain to assist in the presentation and to give the ribbons to the winners. Of course, Kyle would be in command of the photo sessions.

Kyle had asked me to go out with him and told me that he would make reservations at a Copacabana hotel for two nights of our stay in Rio de Janeiro. I thanked him and told him of my date with Sven, but I said that I would see him and Lottie on the beach. We could perhaps have cocktails and do some shopping.

The students and I worked on matting our watercolors. The day before we arrived in Rio, everything was prepared. The invitations for the champagne preview had been printed and put in envelopes under each cabin door. Easels were sent up from the storage room and a large sign was painted that read "Roosevelt Art Gallery." Ballot sheets for the judging were readied. After all was done, I found myself by the pool, enjoying a little rest in a chaise lounge. I closed my eyes and let myself dream of the Rio of my imagination, of the man I loved and with whom I would see Rio for the first time. It was magic!

The next morning I awoke at dawn to not miss the first sight of the Bay of Rio. We arrived on a misty morning to view the lovely hills, the silhouette of Corcovado, with the white statue of Christ the Redeemer dominating the Bay of Rio, Copacabana, the hotels, and the beach a distant gleaming white in the rising sun. The ship docked and the first breakfast bell rang. I went to the dining room and saw a large number of passengers sitting at their tables, finishing their breakfasts. They were going on a tour to Brazilia, the Capital. After breakfast and immigration, I returned to my cabin to eagerly await Sven's call. It came at nine thirty. I was to meet him that afternoon at four, outside the dock's gates. It was all very discreet and at that time of the afternoon, most of the passengers and crew would have left the ship, so chances were that no one would see us. Sven didn't want to have people gossip, since he was the next in command of our ship.

I busied myself with preparation for the art exhibit and took a walk on deck to view the lovely harbor of Rio. I went back to my cabin, not knowing what to do while I waited for the afternoon. Kyle knocked at my door when we came into port, as he usually did. He asked if I wanted to go ashore to Rio Branco to do some shopping. I acquiesced and we took a cab from the swarming docks to Rio Branco. There we walked to a few stores selling souvenirs made of lovely azure blue butterflies. I purchased a chess set, some semi-precious stone necklaces and other trinkets, and some Brazilian tapes. We next went to Copacabana, to Stern's, to view the beautiful jewelry and saw an older couple from the ship buying jewelry of precious stones. Then we returned to the ship.

I took a short nap as the heat and humidity had tired me. After a cool shower, it was almost time to meet Sven. I dressed in my white chiffon gown and high heel shoes of gold, put on my makeup carefully, picked up my gold lame bag, which matched my shoes, and walked out on the crew gangplank amidst the catcalls of the crew members posted at the hole of the ship, as they took care of the cargo, cases of vegetables and fruits. I arrived at the gates a few minutes to four. Sven arrived promptly, dressed in a light gray suit and tie, a white shirt, his blond hair shining in the sun, his serious blue eyes detailing every inch of me with a smile on his lips.

As we walked out of the terminal hand in hand, a dark-skinned, garishly dressed prostitute approached him and spoke boldly a few words of Portuguese. She sent dark flashy looks toward me, but we both ignored her. Later Sven told me that she said in her tongue, "Get rid of your wife. I'll give you a good time." I laughed and took it as a compliment that she thought that I was Sven's wife. We then took a taxi and drove through the streets to Rio Branco and on toward Copacabana and our destination.

We passed lovely beaches, hotels, apartments, buildings, LeBlon Beach and Ipanema. Then we started to climb a hill and I saw small children playing, chickens, a goat, some broken down-shacks. These were the "favelas," the poor sections of Rio. As we climbed higher, there were lovely trees, flowers, and as I looked behind, the Bay of Rio spread before my enchanted eyes. It was so intoxicating being near Sven, so handsome in his civilian clothes, smelling his aftershave lotion, his tan skin shining in the tropical sun, his light blue eyes, hands so supple and caressing. I was thrilled and excited as the taxi climbed higher and higher. I saw more flamboyant trees, flowers, bougainvillaeas, jacaranda, lush palms.

We finally arrived at the Hotel Paradiso, a large modern structure in a state of near completion. We walked through the red-carpeted entrance into the marble hall, past the concierge, to take the elevator to the top, the sixteenth floor. We stepped out into a large open area dominated by an illuminated pool, surrounded by tables covered with white tablecloths and flowers. Brazilian music was playing. Men were dressed in dinner jackets, ladies in cocktail dresses. A fragrant breeze filled the air. My white chiffon dress set off my deep gold tan, and my shiny dark hair was coiffed in an artful chignon. Sven was so tall and fair. We walked to our table, following the maître d'. I noticed all eyes on us.

Our table faced the magnificent view of the Bay of Rio de Janeiro with the jewel-like light setting of Diamants. Sven ordered a bottle of champagne, but the waiter brought us a magnum. Sven told the waiter to leave the bottle at our table. Our dinner was sumptuous, served on china plates. The atmosphere was very romantic, so much like my imagination. Our conversation turned to the voyage, to the many more ports of call, to the passengers. Sven avoided being too personal. I had wished to hear some small words of endearment, but Sven was noncommittal, rather formal. The thought crossed my mind that he was not used to the regal setting, such elegance. Perhaps he was more at ease in simple surroundings. We left, after dancing on the small patio to a Brazilian samba. Sven was still not at ease, being rather stiff.

I had drunk the champagne with gusto and was giddy and light, on the return to Copacabana. I had wanted to see a show or spectacle so we stopped at a large club where a variety show was in progress to a samba beat. We squeezed ourselves around a small table, and watched as scintillating show girls, shaking to the Afro-Brazilian beat, danced on stage, scantily clad, as their golden dark skin glistened with perspiration. The perfection of their bodies, the exciting sensual rhythm of the songs and music excited me, and I was eager to be in Sven's arms.

We returned to the ship as the velvety night of Brazil enveloped us. We went to Sven's quarters. It was four in the morning and all was quiet on board, passengers sleeping in their cabins, the officers, staff and crew probably out still for Brazilian fiesta. In Sven's embrace I became erotic; he lay still on his bed. I kissed all parts of his body, my feverish tongue on his chest, arms, hands. Gently, I became an erotic tool, putting touches here and there softly, trying to arouse him. He was a challenge to me, calm and controlled in his Nordic demeanor. When I finally arrived below his stomach, he started to sigh, and I knew he was ready. I was very excited and wet. I covered his long, hard penis with my mouth and gently pushed a few inches back and forth. Suddenly he grabbed my arms and pulled me over and I lay on top of him, he inside me. We made love passionately and climaxed together.

Afterwards we lay exhausted side by side, a little crowded in his bunk. I fell asleep and woke up to see six o'clock on the alarm clock. Sven was awake, smoking a cigarette. I dressed rapidly and gently kissed his lips, he returned the kiss and I left on tip toes down the stair way through the water-tight doors down the decks below, to my cabin.

The next day was to be our last in Rio and I eagerly awaited Sven's call before going down to have breakfast. The call came at 9 A.M. Sven couldn't see me today as he had duty all day and evening. I became jealous and suspected him of having a date, probably with one of the nurses who were friend-ly with all the officers. We had made tentative plans to go to the beach and take a ride to Corcovado together. I was upset and very unhappy to the point of crying. My nerves were on edge. I put down the receiver and, with tears in my eyes, frustration overcame me. Everything had been so wonderful, then this rejection. It was hard for me to accept. I had told Sven more than once that I loved him, he accepted my declaration with tender kisses and gentle words, but never said he loved me. However, I knew I was the only girl he was with. An officer in his position couldn't afford to jeopardize his career. I respected him and was willing to wait, but being in the throes of jealousy I was blind and dejected.

I put on a light dress, threw a bikini and some toiletries in my American President Line bag, took my camera and my purse, and went down two decks below to Lottie's quarters, which she shared with two of the other beauticians. She wasn't there. I then went to the photo shop and ran into Kyle, who grabbed my arm, saying he had a taxi waiting to take him to the Ouro Verde Hotel on Copacabana. I told him I could join him as I wanted to see the beach. We drove to the hotel and I changed into my bikini while Kyle was fixing himself a cocktail on the terrace, which overlooked the beach. The hotel was small and functional. When I was ready for the beach I went downstairs and out of the hotel into the hot sun. Walking on the lovely wide promenade with its black and white arabesque, I crossed the street to the crowded, sandy beach. I found a spot near a family who had planted an umbrella. It was terribly hot and humid. I put a towel over my head, turban-like, and laid a white towel on the sand. I sat for a few minutes, gradually melting in the heat of the sun, as my frustration and anger over Sven dissipated. After awhile I got up and took a walk on the cool sand by the water. As I bent to fix my turban, I noticed a tall man looking at me. He approached and spoke a few words of Portuguese. I answered in French and we began to chat amiably as one native Cariocan to a tourist. As we both sat on my small towel, I found him serious-looking even in his white swimming trunks. Not being able to speak Portuguese fluently, I couldn't talk to him. After saying goodbye, I left the beach.

I returned to the hotel and knocked on the door of Kyle's room. He opened it with a tall glass of bourbon on ice in one hand, and I saw his camera on a tripod on the balcony facing the beach. Kyle told me practically every move I had made in the hour I was on the beach and told me that he took many photos of me, particularly ones of me talking to the stranger on the beach at Copacabana. Kyle was a little naughty and certainly a voyeur.

After dressing, I left again and went shopping, stopped at Stern's jewelry store on Copacabana, where I saw many of the passengers from the ship. I bought a small gold ring with tiny diamonds shaped like a flower. Later, on Rio Branco again, I bought Brazilian tapes, souvenirs, and when I returned to Copacabana, I saw at a terrace café some crew members sitting in the shade. Lottie was among them. I told her about Kyle having a room at Ouro Verde and that we could change our clothes and rest. So we both returned to Kyle's hotel and had more drinks.

While I had both of their undivided attentions, I gave Lottie and Kyle an account of my time with Sven and his "desertion" this last day. I started to cry shamelessly and told them of my unhappiness. They knew that I was in love with Sven and Lottie was sympathetic, Kyle merely sarcastic. The alcohol was affecting everyone differently. It made me sad. Kyle became amorous, and started to fondle Lottie. It was getting dark. We decided to get some fresh air. We left and walked to Copacabana again, admiring the fantastic scenery of Corcovado, the gentle hills, and the lights. Later we went back to the room. I lay on the sofa and fell asleep. When I awoke, it was daylight and Kyle and

Lottie were fresh and ready to go back to the ship. I took my bag over my shoulder and we all piled in a taxi. Loaded with our purchases, we returned to the ship as dawn and a light breeze welcomed us. I was rested and reflected briefly on those two days and nights of my first visit to Rio, where I had this most romantic night with Sven. I thought of the blue indigo of the hills, the green aqua waters, the golden evening lights. Later, I painted a picture from imagination of my impressions of Rio de Janeiro at night, Ipanema, Sugar Loaf, the Christ statue at Corcovado. . .

The passengers' art exhibit was a hit. Many ribbons were awarded. The voting kept everyone who was not an artist busy. All were in excellent moods. Hors d'oeuvres and champagne were served. The jovial captain pinned ribbons on watercolors while the ever-present Kyle took pictures of the captain, artists, and teacher. The sailing was smooth. The chief purser orchestrated the event. Every one was elated by their visit to Rio. Small groups with their watercolors under their arms returned to their cabins. The judges with ballot sheets in hand were rewarded with more champagne and photo snapping. The easels were returned to storage and classes were to resume the next day. Our voyage was progressing and our next port was Montevideo, Uruguay, two days away.

The city of Montevideo was very European in flavor with many lovely parks and magnificent equestrian statues in bronze. Around the plaza were shops with leather goods and factories. After World War II the people who came to Montevideo were a mixture of Europeans. Rio Plata was a large body of water, which we sailed next.

The next day, we anchored in the port of Buenos Aires, Argentina. I was looking forward to visiting this much heralded city, strolling on Calle Florida with its smart boutiques and cafés. The district of la Bocca had very much an Italianate flavor. I spent a couple of delightful hours in the Viejo Almacen, a place of tango singers, redolent of yesteryears, so romantic and picturesque. The houses in the Barrio la Bocca were garishly decorated. I walked endlessly on that first day. I came upon a small square surrounded by large acacia trees. It reminded me of old Montmartre in Paris. A flea market was in progress. Trinkets, oddities, a Spanish mantilla, antique jewelry, copper, china, all tempted me. I bought a lot of malachite beads which I thought I would string for a necklace. I knew I paid too much for the beads, but I was so taken by the atmosphere.

After taking a few photos, I returned to the ship as that evening a group of Argentinian tango dancers was to perform for the pleasure of the passengers. Standing in the corner with my sketchbook propped against a chair, I began to work with a pen and ink to draw the sinuous movements of the slim dancers performing to the tango music, as the bandoneon and accordion played in concert. There was much energy during the lasso dance with a couple of gauchos. I worked fast, putting touches of watercolors here and there, drawing the costumes accurately. From time to time, I sensed curious passengers looking over my shoulder with appreciative comments. The music was exciting and it was with a feeling of satisfaction that I went to my cabin, putting the sketches neatly in a pile, next to my sketchbooks and watercolors from the various ports of call on this voyage.

In the morning we sailed to our next destination, the straits of Magellan, that incredible zone of ever-changing lights, four or five times from day to night in a single 24-hour period. Our cruise in the straits was to be a long, long day and very cold. I bundled up in heavy woolen sweaters I had purchased in Montevideo and went up on deck. No classes were held today. Everyone was on deck to view the fascinating spectacle on each side of the ship: stark, rocky mountains, gray and grim, covered with snow. Here and there were occasional strange flares, like flames, as we quickly passed. It was stark and inhospitable, no birds or trees, total silence, the sky gray with white clouds. We sailed gingerly through the dark waters. Our Chilean pilot, who had boarded in Buenos Aires, guided the ship slowly through the narrowest passageways.

Meanwhile, some merriment was happening on the deck below where the swimming pool was located. Through a dense fog, I located a group of hardy swimmers, gray haired men and women, about a dozen, frolicking happily in the heated pool, enjoying themselves. You could see the vapor rising from the pool to mix with the icy air. The jolly group was given large glasses of hot rum while the chief steward supervised this exhilarating fun of those courageous passengers, aptly called "the Penguins' Club." As I pulled the collar of my parka closer to my neck, I caught a glimpse of Sven on the lookout bridge, a stern expression on his face, looking at the threatening skies. A flurry of snow and wind added to the merriment of the swimmers who were jostling each other in the pool.

I retired to the warm lounge at tea time and after a cup of hot tea, I quickly went back on deck after stopping in my cabin to fetch my sketchbook and sepia pens. I positioned myself not to miss the two huge mountainous rocks in the distance and started to draw the forms and outline of the rocks, and the sea. The railing of the ship served as my easel. I worked fast before my fingers numbed, but I kept on working as we approached closer. Suddenly the skies darkened and for about fifteen minutes it was like night. You could only distinguish the mass of rock in the distance, no details in this eerie light. On the horizon, ahead of the ship, was a streak of lights and as we passed it the skies were blue again and heavy with clouds like white puffs. At cocktail time, the bar was buzzing with excited voices. All day long we had been briefed by the Chilean pilot of our passage through the straits; he gave us the history of the Straits of Magellan. I remember the sight of the haunting carcass of a cruise ship sunk on the reefs. As I was engrossed with my sketching, Kyle took some photos of me in action.

Dinnertime was cheerful. I had done some good sketches in spite of my frozen fingers. I couldn't draw with my gloves on. The small cabin, crowded now with my many purchases during the trip, was warm and cozy. I slept well. The next morning I awoke and the ship was still. After a magical day and night in the Straits of Magellan we had anchored near the small town of Puerto Montt Chile. The weather was still cool. After the formalities, I walked on the pier of this tiny harbor. It looked like a small fishing village in Portugal, gaily colored boats bobbing near the pier. The morning passed very rapidly, nothing to buy as the town was very poor. We were on the high seas en route to Valparaiso and Vina del Mar.

I had heard so much about the resort of Vina del Mar that I was slightly disappointed. The main streets, uninteresting shops, an old but remodeled casino, with a sad façade: there was nothing of consequence to remember. Valparaiso was more to my liking. It was a small port town with hills and lovely sea views, and appetizing sea food restaurants. The Chileans were friendly and curious about Americans. We tried the exceptionally strong-bodied Chilean wine. The curio shops in the harbor of Valparaiso were full of copperware and lapis stone jewelry. The cargo ships on the docks were loaded with crates of apples and coffee beans in large sacks bursting with aroma. Another day at sea and we arrived in the port of Antofagasta. Chile is well known for its guano and salt deposits. It was eerie to drive through the black desert sand to see the guano and the factories processing it. Chile possessed marvelous lakes and Alpine scenery, but we didn't see them as we were only on the coastline.

The next port was totally different. We were in Ecuador in the port of Guayaquil. Here, I felt, was the exotic, the different. The tour of the city on a rickety bus was harrowing. We arrived at a museum, which was truly fascinating. Among the many artifacts made by the Ecuadorian Indians, was a shrunken human head, the size of a small fist, in a glass case. It still had a full head of hair, the mouth was sewn tight, the skin turned dark and leathery. Next we visited the cemetery, which was most interesting because of the marble statuary, well chiseled by stone cutters mostly from Europe, as many of the early immigrants of Ecuador were of European extraction. Almost every day we were in a different port around South America. My classes had concluded, but I was preparing for my own personal art exhibit before we returned to homeport from our Round the World voyage. The students and passengers were curious to see my paintings. The theme of my show was "Faces and Places Around the World."

I had prepared about twenty-five watercolors and twenty-five oils for my exhibit. I was putting on final touches, late in my cabin after we left various ports. My collection was a wide variety of watercolors showing Hong Kong, dancers from Ceylon, Jaipur street scenes, temples of Kyoto, African women, tea planters, and Indian children with large eyes. We still had Peru, Colombia, the Panama Canal, and Mexico to go for me to add to my impressionistic collection.

After we sailed from Ecuador, we were two days at sea with our next port Lima, Peru. I was very excited at the prospect of seeing Machu Picchu but, alas, I never got there. A tour was being set up for the passengers, an overnight tour of about thirty-five people. I was asked again to be an escort on the tour. After we anchored in the port of Callao, our small group was driven to Lima airport for the one-hour flight to Cuxco. The plane was late and as we waited at the airport terminal, I saw Indian women with baskets and children tied to their backs with strong colorful shawls on their heads. They wore strange white hats shaped like panamas, but higher, with wide ribbons around their long shiny black hair, which hung in a single braid. Some Indians had cages with chickens. A boy led a pig by a rope around its neck. All this jolly group was aboard the plane when it arrived three hours late. Our group was seated in the first rows, while the others were arranged pell-mell in the back of the aircraft. We departed and as the plane ascended, the vista of the city of Lima spread below. We climbed to a higher altitude and soon were flying over the snow-capped Andes Mountains with plains and rivers below. It was the Vilcabamba Valley. We were enroute to Cuxco several thousand feet above sea level. The plane was flying only by visibility, no radar.

We arrived in Cuxco in the early evening. A pale sky greeted our group, which was met by a small bus and we proceeded to our inn, where we would lodge for the night. It was cold, much colder than Lima. The roads were not paved and the hotel was close to the center of Cuxco. The cathedral was vis-

Market
Cuxco
Peru
were I missed
The Train To Machu Picchu

ible in the center of the large plaza. Our inn was cold and the room sparse, but a large supply of woolen blankets was put on each bed. We were two to a room. After dinner, which was a simple fare, we had a couple of hours to acquaint ourselves with the town. In the early morning, the tour was to take the special train for the seven- to eight-hour trip to Machu Picchu. I took my camera and went for a walk. Near the plaza, I saw men sitting asleep near the protected walls of the cathedral, their heads on their arms, ponchos covering them. The passengers were still at the inn getting adjusted to the high altitude. I thought I was not much affected, but after walking for twenty minutes, I became very tired and returned to the hotel. Some people were sitting by the fire and I joined them for a drink of hot tea. Before we all retired to our rooms the tour guide told us that we were to be up at 5 A.M., and to promptly breakfast and depart at six as our train would not wait. There were only so many hours of daylight. I couldn't find warmth in the narrow bed in spite of the many blankets that I had put over me. I dreamt of the lost city and the spectacular sights that I had seen on so many travel brochures. I woke up, suddenly startled, yet it was still dark. I pulled the curtains back and looked at my watch. It was half past six, I had overslept and the bed next to mine was empty. I rushed downstairs.

All was quiet as everybody had left except one of the officers of the ship who had accompanied the tour. He said if we hurried, we might still catch the train. We took a rickety car that was parked by the hotel. But by the time we got to the station, the train had left. I took my misfortune in stride and decided to explore the city of Cuxco and the surroundings during this suddenly free day. All around the cathedral was a market, women and children squatting on the dirt, selling meager fruits and vegetables that were grown on the slopes of the Andes. Wild pigs were roaming around. I filmed the scene with my 8mm camera. It was very colorful. People wore richly colored ponchos with magenta shawls. Rust, orange with green and black striped ponchos for the men with their hair in pigtails. And on all heads the small white fedora hat, typical of Peru.

Standing by the plaza was a young Peruvian dressed in an alpaca coat. He was motioning me to come. As I came by, I saw a small dark car in which Tom sat, the officer who went with me late to the train. He said that this young guide would take us to Sacsayhuaman to see the ruins and to a tour of the Andean Plateau. I joined them and off we drove, taking a mountainous road to the ruins. We first stopped by a waterfall where Indian women were displaying beautiful llama blankets and ponchos. I purchased a blanket and a couple of small ponchos. Then we left the car and walked up the hill to see the views. We passed some llamas, heavy with burdens on their backs, a young boy guiding them through the mountains. My breath was getting slow; I was having difficulty climbing. As the guide approached me, I noticed him chewing something that I found out was coca leaves. He put a bunch in my hand and told me to inhale them. I did so thinking it would do me no harm. After a while I felt better and was able to rejoin the two men. We had approached the ruins of Sacsayhuaman. with its very impressive, massive square blocks artfully put together to form a long wall. There was a door through which I wandered, in awe. How could men have carried and placed those gigantic stones one on top of the other? It was a beautiful sight. We took some photos. It was getting cold and we were at a very high altitude. The road back was easy. We stopped again at a native Indian market. I bought some lovely replicas of Inca terra cotta statues that I carefully wrapped in my earlier purchases, the ponchos.

The flight back to Lima was uneventful. The passengers were excited about their trip to Machu Picchu. However, the weather had not been good, and the view was hazy. I was not too disappointed, as I had seen some beautiful sights and had made good purchases. I had left something to see for some other future trip.

One more day at sea and we arrived in Cartagena, Colombia, the country of emeralds. Cartagena was an old colonial port, an old fort dominating the sea. There were quiet streets with low houses and lovely wrought-iron balconies. In a beautiful district up the hill, we arrived at an old hotel, covered with bougainvillaea. We stepped into the marbled lobby for a cool drink. Then I was off to the crowded popular district, where I purchased Colombian cassettes and records. Near the town, in one of the many jewelry stores selling gold and emeralds, I bought a small ring of rough stones and a tiny necklace of gold chain with a small pendant of one emerald stone, which I was assured was of good quality. That night on board the ship was a dance troupe, a typical Colombian group with their own band. I was sketching the dancers to the rhythms of "Cumbia" and other melodious sounds.

We reached Buenaventura the next day and by contrast it was very poor. Descendants of African slaves live there. We docked in the early morning. A light rain had fallen the night before and the docks were slippery. At dawn, an officer from the engine room was on duty, but no one was around to tie our ship to the docks. The ship was at arm's length from the docks. The gangplank was not put up yet. Robert Bishop, the second officer, thought he could easily cover the short distance by jumping from the ship to the dock. In the pockets of his white overalls, he had some tools. As he came to the edge of the ship, after sliding the rail gate, he then jumped but missed the dock. No one knew what happened next but we were in Bonaventura for three days, trying to recover his body. A team of searchers in scuba diving suits looked under the ship. Apparently, the officer had slipped and fell and maybe hurt his head. With the heavy tools in his pockets he had drowned. We were all pretty shaken. Several native Colombians, in their canoes, were also in the search party, going out to sea, with long hooks to try to find the body. On the third day, everyone was on deck to watch these goings on when at last the canoe with the natives brought a body to the surface. It was Robert, an awful sight. I took a quick glance at the bloated, white-suited body. I was not able to stay on deck any longer. Arrangements were made to fly the body home before we departed from Buenaventura, a port I will not remember fondly.

The weather was constantly hot and extremely humid. As we approached the Panama Canal, it took all day sailing through locks from Cristobal to Panama City. Everyone went ashore, mostly to the Hilton Panama Hotel and Casino. I put a few coins in the slot machines but soon left to explore the city.

Panama City was a sprawling, lovely city. Everyone it seemed understood English. A large US military base existed there in 1968. I was most interested in going to San Blas to see the Cunas Indians, but I didn't take the tour. I was afraid of the mosquito-infested islands. Instead I went to the native market and bought Cunas embroideries and artifacts. A lovely buffet was served on deck to all the passengers and, at sea again, we reached Colon, then the Gulf of Mexico and Acapulco.

There were two days to rest and finish preparations for my art exhibit, which was to be held as we left Acapulco. Sven called and I sensed, with the voyage coming to an end, that the next few days were to be our last together. We met and took the boat ashore to Acapulco. Drinks on the beach, nights of love, very poignant as I lay with my head on his chest. Time passed quickly. The hot sand, the sun, the white hotels, cruise liners at anchor. At night on deck, Acapulco was aglow with a million lights in the indigo sky. As we smoothly sailed the next morning, I set up my art exhibit with anticipation, and placed invitations under the cabin doors of all the passengers. The exhibit was a great success: many sales, photo sessions, congratulations from everyone, a large variety of paintings in oil, watercolors and sketches. I was elated with the success of the exhibit and the knowledge that I would see my darling son Gregg in a few days.

In Puerto Vallarta and picturesque Manzanillo, we stopped briefly to see Las Hadas, a Moorish setting amidst jungle-like swamps, poverty, and shacks. We shopped for souvenirs. Kyle, Lottie, and a few friends had a party, one of many celebrations. At the captain's farewellparty everyone was in evening gowns or tuxedos. Caviar, champagne, music, and dancing completed the mood. The weather grew warm as we approached our final visitation port, San Pedro.

We docked in the port of Los Angeles, where many passengers left the ship. Finally, on a glorious January day under clear blue skies, we sailed under the Golden Gate Bridge to the pier where Gregg and Lillian awaited me.

Chapter Six

I WAS OVERJOYED to be back home in San Francisco, spending time with my son and relating my trip to him. The time passed quickly.

Five days later, I was back on the same ship for another trip around the world. Different places, different crew and staff. On this next voyage a distinguished gentleman gave me much attention. A widower, he was chief surgeon of a hospital in Alabama. We made a rendezvous in a discreet manner; we found ourselves attracted to each other. We had left Gibraltar and the ship would sail to Lisbon, Portugal, then cruise for five days in the Mediterranean and wind up in Southampton, England. Then, on to the Bahamas and around the world. I had asked for a short leave of absence to see my cousins in London, and I was granted permission to leave the ship in Lisbon and rejoin it in Southampton. Dr. Gerhard Welsh was a medium-sized man in his early sixties, with a handsome head of white hair. With a maximum discretion we arranged to fly on the same plane out of Lisbon to Paris. We had plans to meet at the Plaza Athenée Hotel. On the flight we were among other passengers from the ship, so we tried to ignore each other. It was thrilling to me, this adventure. I knew he would be kind to me. His manners were gentle, and I liked his smiling blue eyes. We arrived in Paris in a snowstorm. All was white around us, and it was a relief to be in the luxurious hotel suite, with adjoining rooms. I prepared myself to be attractive for an evening of dinner and early rest. The next day in Paris, Gerhard and I went on a shopping spree. I purchased a lovely pair of boots, a white pantsuit of wool, and lingerie. We dined in the hotel dining room and went back to our suite. What I remember of that night was that Gerhard was surprisingly virile. Later I learned he had had a penile implant! London was cold, as was our room at the Dorchester. We boarded our ship in Southampton for the next leg of our cruise around the world. I saw Gerhard again in Los Angeles, on a weekend in the spring. We stayed good friends. After 1969, I cruised around the world five more times

often I took Gregg
on cruises, while I
worked as Art instructor

and would sail a total of thirty-eight cruises until 1980. On some cruises I took Gregg with me.

When I returned to San Francisco, regular life resumed. Gregg was still in military academy and we now lived in Palo Alto. I would go to San Francisco, where I saw my friend Benny Bufano, the sculptor. I remember his studio, a vast cluttered warehouse on Minna Street, and Benny in the middle of unfinished sculptures, statues, mosaics in various stages of completion. Some works in marble were so large they loomed over the tiny sculptor. To the right of the large space was a wooden door leading to a stairway. One room was at the top where a sign read "Henry Miller's Room," with stacks of books on the floor and shelves. The second room was sparse: in a small alcove was space for cooking, with utensils, a wok, some pans, and opposite was a spartan couch. Above the couch there was a serigraph of the "Black Cat." The other small room had a cot with Indian blankets on it, on the wall photographs of statues of Buddha and oriental figures. Bufano slept there. I often sat on the little couch in this room with Benny, talking for hours. I felt it was a great privilege to be there. It was very stuffy at times, but I was enlightened to great secrets. I remember during one visit Benny decided to cook us some lunch, a strange concoction of black mushrooms. Bufano would take me occasionally to Japan Center to eat sushi, sashimi, and tempura. Once we went to Trader Vic's on Cosmo Alley. While we ate, he would stuff his pockets with crackers to feed the birds; such a gentleman. Benny also had a small studio at the Press Club on Post Street. After an outing in the evening, he would take me home in a taxi, then walk home. Benny was a great talker. We often spoke Italian and I would mix in some French words. He would telephone two or three times a day or to ask me when we had a date, as sometimes he couldn't remember. Returning home from a trip to Italy, Bufano brought a small silver knife and fork from the plane as a souvenir for my nine-year-old son.

I wanted to meet with Henry Miller, Benny's friend, and Benny told me he would arrange it. He telephoned me the next day, saying, "It is all arranged." And I answered, "When can we go?" My friend Galina would drive us. We left, the three of us, early the next morning, bound for Los Angeles. When we arrived in Century City, we rested in a motel. We were all tired except Benny, who refused the twin bed and slept on the floor while we girls used the beds.

Around noon the next day, we arrived at 444 Ocampo Drive in Pacific Palisades and rang the doorbell. A distinguished man opened the door to let us in. Recognizing Benny, he seemed surprised at our visit and explained that

Mr. Miller was in Paris and had been there for several weeks on the set of the film *Quiet Days at Clichy*, on which he was a consultant.

Bufano, not shaken at all and with amazing calm, said that it was a mistake. Henry was probably riding his bicycle and will return shortly. With aplomb, Benny proceeded to show us the house, swimming pool, various rooms, Miller's studio, and library with his books, translated into many languages, paintings, watercolors by himself, photographs, a large picture of Miller. I took many snapshots. We sat by the pool and a young woman brought us drinks and sandwiches. Before leaving we thanked the man, who gave me a copy of Miller's book *Remember to Remember*, in which there is a chapter about Bufano. In Miller's bedroom was a wall where Benny signed his name. I added mine. I noticed photos of young children, Miller's family. Time and space meant nothing to Benny. In that respect, he was like Einstein. In his mind he had arranged it all, and there was an explanation of his wonderful character. I saw Henry Miller only in my mind and imagination. What Benny did was to actualize my desire to be in the presence of Henry Miller's art and essence. As to Bufano himself, the artist, the man, "Grateful is sleep but more to be of stone, where ruins and dishonor reign." Those were Benny's words, written to a dear nun whom in his youth he had loved and admired.

Benny Bufano was born in San Félé in 1889, a small village near Rome. His life ended in a tiny room atop a sculptor's studio cluttered with books, in San Francisco. The year was 1971. My friendship with Benny had begun four years prior and continued when I returned from my first trip around the world, as artist and language director on the cruise line. We had several meetings and conversations about art, travels and love of Bali, also philosophy and affairs of the world. I would dwell on Bali, as it was then, my Shangri-la. Bufano had lived in Java and had deep feelings about its people, beauty and art. I became his confidant, more than a friend. He often told me about a young woman who tormented him. Her name was Serena. She was beautiful and demanding and at times very cruel. Benny could love many women in different ways and on different levels. He needed the adulation of friends.

During my travels, I found most of my inspirations to paint came from the Orient, having had strong inclinations toward Japanese, Indonesian, Malaysian and Hindu art and sculptures. I would paint many subjects and scenes of my trip and have art exhibits on shipboard. At many of the ports of call a letter or a card from Bufano would greet me. "To mia carissima Nadine, the sunshine of San Francisco is in full bloom. Not a cloud in the sky overhead. So this is a cheerful wish. How are you, beautiful one? With love in the sun, Benny."

In the beginning of 1970 I received this card: "My dear Nadine, this card will reach you in Colombo, Ceylon around 30th of January. Advise me of your stops where I can reach you. I will try to contact you, wherever you are. As you must know, I miss you. B. Bufano."

Another card, "Dear Nadine, this will catch you at Cape Town, waiting to greet you on your long and belated trip. I may be in Los Angeles, when you reach there, as I have an exhibit there. God bless you. Be of good cheer. Benny."

Later that trip, when we reached Singapore, a card: "My dear Nadine, how are you? Thank for your card from Nicco. Nicco, beautiful place with beautiful temples! (Nikko, Japan, was misspelled) I will send this card to Singapore, and the next to Colombo and Bombay. I was there. May the great spirit of God bless you. Benny."

Many numerous, endearing letters and cards, full of love and caring would greet me. I was always looking eagerly under my cabin door on the ship to see the mail when we arrived in a port. Letters from my little son Gregg and Benny were all my joy!

Benny was keenly interested in astrology. He instinctively felt a relationship with the stars in heaven and their influence on humans. Here is a poem he wrote in his youth:

Gia. Like shooting stars, we wander in space whirling and spinning like a top in a dream.
But too quickly we come to crash into the whirlpool and in a flash we whirl into a furnace of death.

Not all his poems were so gloomy and foreboding. Here is a lovely one, found in an old notebook:

I wander in the fields. I meet the flowers, I meet the trees. I bathe my feet in running
brooks, and love the flowers, birds and trees.

And children basking in the sun. I love their little bodies, browned by the warm sun and
kissed by the flowers, blackened by the earth and washed by the rain.

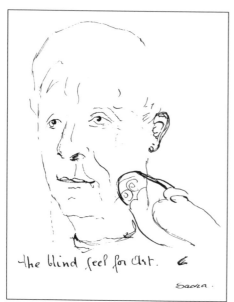

the blind feel for Art.

Sadra.

living with the Coolies in the
famous potteries of Shahuan China,
I found Buddha ....

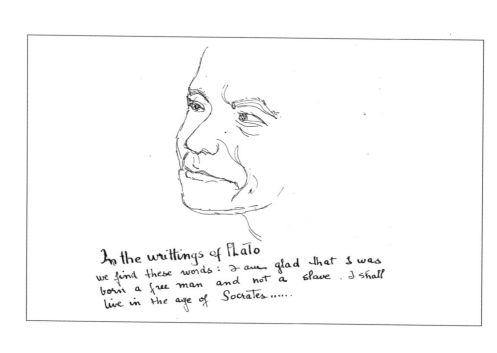

In the writtings of Plato
we find these words: I am glad that I was
born a free man and not a slave. I shall
live in the age of Socrates......

Otto Preminger, friend of Bufano

the man of hard materials
is soft and Gentle...
Sacha

I love to see them kiss the flowers, love the birds, chipmunks, rabbits, fowls, bears, ants
and all the animals of the earth.

I love to see them early to bed and early to rise and sing the melodies with the birds. To
sleep in the fields and under the trees, to revere the heavens and revere the earth, to count
the stars and look at the moon.

Also in that notebook, a quote signed by William Saroyan, "I know some people dislike Bufano. I have talked with some of those people. I haven't been able to understand anything, from what they've said. Because it's been as a rule irrelevant. Many people dislike me too. I am grateful to them. I think Bufano knew the importance of enemies. I think he knows the important thing is to be sure they are wrong! They are! His and mine."

As for Bufano's art, Saroyan wrote in 1937, "Some of Bufano will grip the best spirit in the world and a lot of it will elevate the worst. He is only human."

That last week before he died, on a Tuesday, we had a lunch date at Scoma's on Fisherman's Wharf and it was understood that he would then come to dinner at my home on Friday evening. When Friday came, not hearing from Benny, I called a mutual friend, who told me that perhaps Benny misunderstood and thought it would be Saturday. Benny was unpredictable. Saturday came, no calls. I was scared, sensing something terribly wrong. On Sunday morning I was awakened by a call telling me that Bufano was found dead in his studio! On a foggy day by the Bay in San Francisco, that luncheon at Scoma's was our last meeting.

Recollecting all our meetings, I was under the impression that he would live forever. It was a great shock and greater loss to me.

We would often meet and talk about the "book." Benny was really a frustrated writer. I think he enjoyed having people write about him so he could find out what his image was like to others.

I did several sketches of him, some were good and some not so good. It was understood that I would illustrate his book. I recorded Benny's voice on tape, and also some of his friends' recollections of Benny. I did extensive research. Benny always told me that only another artist could do justice to the "book of his life." Many hours were spent discussing "our book" and ultimately he gave me an enormous pile of archives, notes, photographs, and newspaper articles to help me to illustrate the book. In 1970, while in Tokyo, I went to see Benny's publisher at Weather Hill Publications. I had a letter of introduction signed by Bufano and authorizing me to negotiate on our book. That meeting was brief but very encouraging. Returning home, I kept up my research by listening to his friends, the people who knew him. All of their voices and especially Benny's whispered to me, "Nadine, the strongest creative force is love." We also made a tape while both of us recorded our thoughts at that time. If God wills, there will be more about Bufano in another book.

Several months went by and I continued working on cruise ships, this time to the Orient and the South Pacific. It was on that voyage that I met Mark Osborn, the man I was to marry.

In 1974, I was booked to go to the South Pacific on Royal Viking lines for a sixty-day cruise. The ship sailed smoothly through the Golden Gate. It was a new cruise line, one on which I had never sailed previously. The ship was sparkling, modern, with spacious luxurious lounges and bars and dining rooms in shades of green and gold. I had my table assignment and went to the bar, the one with a large window at the bow of the ship. A slightly built man with wavy blond hair and blue eyes was taking notes. He wore the ship's uniform of green and white with a gold insignia on the shoulder. I figured he was the barman and politely asked him for the directions to the main bar. The man in charge of bars and restaurants was a handsome Englishman, who introduced himself as Mr. Mark Osborn, Chief Steward of Bars and Restaurants. I thanked him and noticed a glint of interest in his eyes. On board, the passengers were mostly a mixture of Americans and Australians, and not many young people. The staff was under fifty years old on average and, in comparison to the passengers, looked even younger.

Our first port of call after we left Los Angeles was Papeete, Tahiti. Mark asked me for a date to go ashore in Papeete. We talked about our lives and I found him charming, but slightly ill at ease. My recent breakup with Sven was still heartbreaking. But I was a romantic and was attracted to Mark. We became lovers after we left Sydney. One night, returning from an excursion, he called me and asked me to his cabin for a drink. We embraced and I looked into his blue eyes, perhaps to find Sven's fierce gaze, but Mark's were only gentle and pleading. His body was slight, hairless, and smelled of English tobacco. The moon appeared through the porthole and after gentle lovemaking, we slept in each other's arms.

I had art classes on this sixty-day cruise around the South Pacific. My stu-

New Guinee woman
Breast feeding both
her child and young pig.

dents were mostly Australian and American, middle-aged women and a couple of youngish women with their husbands. I had other friends on the ship. The dance teachers, Carmen and Ira, had been with me on my very first cruise around the world and I considered them as my good luck charms.

Port Moresby in New Guinea was very primitive. Women wove baskets and brown-bodied children sat in the dirt with chickens and piglets. The excursion bus carried us to the mouth of the Sepik River. There were thatched huts and men and women walked carrying bundles, bones in their nostrils. We stopped in a dilapidated village. I saw an albino native woman nursing a black baby on one breast while a small puppy was sucking at her other nipple. Strange sights in this primitive part of the world where civilization seemed to have stopped a thousand years back. I purchased two primitive masks made of ebony wood with cowry shells for eyes. Next, the ship anchored at the small Pacific Island Tonga, where we went ashore on a tender, before setting sail for Bali, Indonesia.

When we reached Bali, Mark and I went ashore together, taking pictures in picturesque villages. We purchased batik cloth. Near us, a woman was wearing a saffron skirt and pink top, a couple of younger women were holding black umbrellas, a cow grazed in front of the little shack. In the center on one temple's ruins, the native men performed the "monkey dance." They sat in a circle with the arms flailing and their voices screeching like monkeys. We were fascinated to watch their shaking and to hear their mesmerizing chants. Mark and I returned to the ship with purchases of exquisitely carved Bali statues and hand-dyed batik.

I was always carrying a sketchbook wherever I went. Kota Kinabalu, Borneo, Malaysia, and in Hong Kong, the shopper's paradise. Mark was working so I went ashore with Ira and Carmen. Life aboard ship was exciting. We were preparing for a Broadway show and I was to do a number with the dancers, a Roaring Twenties revue. I made up a costume of a short white dress, small white cap with a ribbon and a bow, a long feather boa, and two long bead necklaces. The memory albums growing thick were full of wonderful photographs.

Libertine that I was, I had an eye on our ship's good-looking Swedish doctor, but we only saw each other with groups at cocktail parties. He was very sweet to me, but nothing came of it. My art classes were well-received by my jolly group of shipboard travelers. Meanwhile, Mark was getting very amorous, and always had a bottle of good champagne in his cabin. We arrived in Tokyo. Mark and I went ashore and it was cool during the day. We walked hand in hand and stumbled upon a Japanese festival of some sort. Small children were dressed in red and white with little berets, their little round faces smiling. There was always a crowd at all the temples and shrines, and all we could do was snap photos.

For nostalgia's sake, I wanted to relive with Mark my experiences with Sven. In Honolulu, we walked on the beach, sipped drinks at the Royal Hawaiian, watched the flamboyant sunsets until night fell and the torches were lit. The revue with the passengers entertaining was a big hit. The voyage was drawing to a close. I was taken by my feelings for Mark. I had been single for a long time and often wondered if I would ever get remarried. I wanted a more stable life, for me and Gregg. I was in love with Mark and he seemed so easy to get along with. I thought he would be a good companion, perhaps not as passionate as Sven, but stable and caring. However, I still had reservations about how a union would affect my son, since Gregg was very attached to me.

When the ship arrive in San Francisco, I left Mark with words of love. We were sad and didn't want to part. We promised to write each other and make plans. Mark was to make another South Pacific cruise, and a cruise to Europe. Then he was free from his contract and promised to come to California to see me.

It was a joy to be home again even though returning to my routine work was very hard. But I was a mother first and Gregg had thrived, looking sturdy and well-adjusted, going to school while I was away. Lillian and Sam were perfect grandparents and Gregg also saw his father during my cruises.

A month passed. I reread the letters I had received from Mark and was longing to see him. A plot formed in my head. Why not meet the ship and Mark in the port of Amsterdam during his last cruise? I knew he would be terribly surprised to see me. I was longing to be with him. I knew the element of surprise would conquer him, so I arranged for a ticket to fly to Europe.

First, I went to Paris to see my friends from the early days of Malmaison, as I always did. I arranged to be in Amsterdam two days before the ship arrived on its North Cape cruise. It was summer, 1974. I arrived in Amsterdam, got a hotel room overlooking a busy canal, and rested. The next day, I walked in the city and familiarized myself, then took a taxi to the port and rehearsed in my head how I was going to board the ship without Mark knowing about it. The element of surprise had to be perfect.

It turned out as I expected. I walked on the gangplank and onto the ship directly to the bar where I knew Mark would be. I shall never forget the look of disbelief on his face. He greeted me with a warm embrace and he whispered for me to wait a few minutes as he was busy. After a while, as we talked, he told me how he really was totally surprised and happy. He took the rest of the day off and we dined in a candle-lit restaurant in a narrow alley. Then he went to my hotel to spend the night. Mark had gained a new virility and was very amorous. I was thrilled by the adventure.

The next day we explored Amsterdam together, the canals, Anne Frank's house, and took pictures. When it was time to go, I went to see him one last time on board the ship. In his whites, it was uncanny how much he reminded me of Sven . After a last kiss, I left. Now I knew that he wanted me and wanted to marry me.

When I got home, I received many letters from Mark announcing his arrival in San Francisco. I had told everyone that we were going to be married in Reno as soon as possible. Mark arrived with very little baggage except some Balinese carvings and a stereo. I had a small apartment with three bedrooms, one for my studio, one for Gregg and one for my bedroom. At first Gregg was pouting, but he soon became his usual self. I told him that Mark and I would be married and move to a bigger house so we wouldn't all be in each other's way.

The morning of the wedding arrived and we flew to Reno. We stayed at a hotel near the chapel. While Carmen was arranging my hair and Ira filling a glass of Scotch in our suite, Mark had gone to the casino to gamble. Ira served as Mark's best man and Carmen as my bridesmaid. It was a short wedding in a chapel conformed of fast ceremonies, which included flowers, photo session, and pastor. The next morning we flew back to San Francisco. I was Mrs. Mark Osborn.

We settled into a routine. While Gregg went to school, after a hearty breakfast, Mark would play golf and return late in the evening. We dined together. I had expected Mark to look for a position as a manager in a country club, but nothing happened. Money was in short supply. Tension arose. Lovemaking was strained. We didn't have much privacy, but I was not giving up my dream. I had tried to do my best, by suggesting to Mark to actively pursue his search for a position. Six months had gone by and still no job in sight for Mark. He was still gone everyday. We had separate bedrooms now. Things became worse as I suspected Mark was gambling the little money he had brought with him. I knew he wasn't wealthy but at age forty-five and in good physical condition, it was strange that he could not land a job. Finally, after much discussion, nine months after our wedding, we had the marriage annulled. Mark was unhappy and I was sad, but relieved. He made the decision to go to Australia. There he made a fortune and after five years of hard work, went back to England where he bought a restaurant. But I never regretted our annulment, as it was for the best.

I resumed my travels, to South America, this time on Prudential Line. It was a two-month cruise where we went all around South America on a cargo/passenger ship, with only 80 passengers. I would have art classes and participate in the functions of the ship's staff, such as entertainment and sometimes being a guide for the excursions when we reached ports. My cabin was comfortable and I settled into a routine, looking forward to seeing more exotic ports, some that I had visited before, and some that were new. This summer of 1975, I was able to take Gregg, now fifteen years old, with me on this cruise. He was to help in the capacity of junior purser. We left San Francisco, on a typically foggy summer day, for Los Angeles and Mexico, then on through the Panama Canal to Colombia, Cartagena, and Rio. There I had the surprise of my life. Standing on the docks waving frantically at us was my good friend, and "Southern belle," Magnolia, who worked for an airline. She had taken a vacation to surprise me and to join us for a four-day cruise until we reached Buenos Aires. Laughter and cheers followed. Magnolia made lots of friends on board, especially one of the officers. In Buenos Aires, we went ashore together and sampled the wonderful beef of Argentina. We toured Sao Paolo, where I called my friend from Paris, who had invited Gregg and me some years ago to a Seine cruise. Magnolia left us in Buenos Aires and flew home.

The ship continued on toward the Straits of Magellan, stopping only in Mare de Plata to pick up our pilot for the trip through the treacherous waters. The captain was taking movies of the ceremony in which newcomers to the crossing had to undergo a certain ritual by the pool involving an egg on the head, ketchup, and a shampoo of pasta. Gregg was one of the unfortunates who had the treatment, much to the merriment of the other passengers. In Chile, we went to Vina del Mar. We purchased souvenirs and took photos. On board there would be casino night, where we girls of the staff would don costumes of black leotard and boa, lots of legs showing. When a folkloric dance troupe would come on board to entertain the passengers, I would sketch them and later add watercolor touches.

Caracas was a surprisingly clean city. We anchored at Puerto Cabello and the tour bus took us to the city, passing many shanties and shacks along the way. A sumptuous buffet was prepared for us on the return trip at the Hilton

Hotel. Our stay in Venezuela was short, sadly only a day. I remember only the sprawling city of Caracas and the Colonial Hotel in Avila up on the hills.

Our next stop was Callao, the port of Lima in Peru. I loved Peru. Mostly the people had tanned faces under their round hats and covered with ponchos of various colors. In Cuxco again, I filmed the Indian market with my 8mm camera, as always. Gregg kept a diary and wrote some observations every day.

In San Francisco I would try to see Benny Bufano as often as possible. I remember his words to me on our last meeting, "You must take care of the flower garden." This sentence haunts me to this day. In his archives, which he gave to me to write "his book", I found many references to the "flower garden." Benny Bufano died alone in his studio. Most of San Francisco's well-known personalities attended the solemn funeral at St. Patrick's Cathedral. The papers and some other artwork that Benny gave me stayed in the bank vault for more than twenty years.

At a party, I think it was at the Russian Embassy, I met a handsome, tall, soft-spoken man named Dexter Cross. We found out that we had much in common. Dexter was in his mid-forties, with an athletic build, a sensual mouth, and a lovely head of curly brown hair. Dexter was an art appraiser and dealer, which interested me. We met several times and became close. I often accompanied him on his appraisals, during which I learned about 19th and 20th century paintings. I learned the value of a Corot or a Delacroix sketch and also some more contemporary artists. It added dimension to my knowledge of art. I read a lot of art books, mostly the Impressionists, which I was very fond of, and I did some paintings in the style of Monet and Renoir.

Dexter was married, with children, living with them outside of San Francisco. I was still living in my apartment in Palo Alto while Gregg was in high school. Dexter and I frequently saw each other, and became lovers. I admired him very much and was terribly infatuated with him. We could not be together in my apartment because of my son and, of course, he had to return home to his family. So we rented an apartment in San Francisco. It was very convenient for Dexter's business and also for us to be together. We spent many weekends in the apartment, making love, talking, and exploring our senses and feelings. Dexter was tender and I loved his touch and his strong, tanned body. He claimed to be of Indian blood, but his looks were more Latin.

At that time, the 1970s, the sex revolution was in full swing. Dexter and I found ourselves going to various parties where one could have many partners in one evening. While food and liquor were always served, drugs were generally absent. On rare occasions, people might have a marijuana cigarette.

I was not at all attracted to the drug or sex scene, but I accompanied Dexter, because I was much in love with him and did not want to lose him. I never pretended to be aroused by the naked bodies at some of those parties and I would view the scene, detached, as an artist. While Dexter was engaging in amorous sensual exercises with one or two girls, I was but a voyeur. It was usually in a comfortable, upper class home, mostly in the suburbs of San Francisco. No one knew about AIDS in those days. Sometimes a handsome young man would make advances toward me. I merely let him caress my bosom, but felt it would be too hypocritical to have any more contact, as I had no feeling for him.

This went on for a year or so. Sometimes we would go to the hot tubs or mixed baths, south of San Francisco. We also went to nude beaches. The sex scene was in full swing. I felt disgusted and told Dexter so, but I was desperately hanging on to him. I felt that he was taking great risks with his life, risks that caught up with him later. We would go together to gallery openings and return to our little apartment. On weekdays, I would be home with Gregg while Dexter would be at his business and with his family.

I was called to another cruise to South America and it was a welcome change for the next few months. I came home and was glad to see Gregg. A new shopping center was built next to Palo Alto. I opened a small studio and started to paint portraits and sell some of my paintings. It was successful and I was now making good money. My cruises around the world were winding down, and the Prudential line seldom hired me for its cruises around South America. I took time off to paint and spent time with Gregg.

After a year had gone by, I had just returned from Paris after a two-month stay in Europe. The little shopping center gallery in the university town where I lived had been closed since it was summer and business was slow. It was good to be back home in my cozy apartment. Gregg, still in high school, was a strapping youth of seventeen. It was sultry and hot that fall and I was spending lazy days on the chaise lounge on the sun deck, reminiscing about my Parisian romance.

I first saw the young man from a St. Germain café, where I was sitting on the terrace sipping a drink. He walked by nonchalantly, looking boldly at me. I did not avoid his glance. I was a student of humanity, an artist, and also a tourist looking for distractions! I had to call on my friend Lyvia, who had an apartment in Paris. As I walked past the tables to go downstairs to a telephone, I saw that the young man had taken a seat directly behind me at a small table and had ordered a cup of coffee. I returned from the telephone, not having gotten an answer. The terrace had a large window and in it, I could see in the reflection the man behind me. He was in his early thirties, slight of build, and dressed in khakis with a smart safari jacket and tan slacks. He had the look of the usual wolf on the prowl. I noticed his fine, Italian, dark burgundy shoes and his black silk socks. He had a devilishly appealing smile and he didn't seem to notice that his reflection was being observed in the window.

I left the café, starting to walk to the Metro St. Germain. Standing in line to buy my ticket, I sensed I was being watched. Turning around, I saw the young man grinning. Coyly, I said, "Are you following me?" He replied that he had been looking at me in the café and in a cavalier fashion asked me to have a drink with him. His manners were good and he had a neat appearance. Before I acquiesced, I told him that I had very little time, because I was going to see a friend. We sat outside Café Mabillon and chatted amiably. He was amused by my description of life in California. To him it was still the far, far West. His only voyage had been to New York for a brief visit. He spoke passable English and told me he was on vacation for another week. I excused myself and tried the telephone again, this time getting an answer and an invitation to dinner from Lyvia.

The young man's name was Alain. He offered to drive me to Neuilly, a plush residential district where my friend lived. As we drove, he began to press me for a rendezvous. I agreed to meet him the next day for a dinner date. It was late August, and I was staying at my small hotel near Etoile on Avenue Victor-Hugo. In a few days I would be flying home. Alain arrived at seven o'clock, looking smart in a light tan suit, white shirt, and tie. We dined by candlelight in a small restaurant on the Isle St. Louis. We walked along the Seine and sat on a bench. He drew me near and we kissed. I liked the feel of his soft lips and the touch of his well-manicured hands. The place was nearly deserted, but it felt like summer as the trees had green foliage. I felt slightly foolish and carefree. I saw us as anonymous young lovers by the Seine, just like in the French songs. We drove back to my hotel and I kissed him lightly on the cheek, thanking him for the lovely evening.

The next day, Alain came to fetch me and we took a stroll in the Bois de Boulogne. I had on a summery dress, and Alain wore a light shirt opened generously on his chest. He smelled of Pino Sylvestre cologne. His hand felt dry in my moist palm. I was nervous. We arrived at a clearing in the woods and there on the grass we kissed passionately. This new passion was very exciting to me. Before we went too far, I told him to stop, that we should postpone something inevitable.

That evening, after a light dinner in a neighborhood bistro, Alain showed me his apartment, two rooms with kitchen and bathroom, in a modern building, near the Eiffel Tower. It was decorated soberly in dark brown tones. The living room had a large couch in a suede-like fabric. On the walls were antique photographs in rococo frames of women in languid poses in turn-of-the-century fashion. Alain uncorked a bottle of Mumm's while I sat on the couch. I sipped the champagne slowly. Alain, standing, was watching me, grinning his devilish grin. As he inserted tapes into the stereo, the room suddenly rocked with Brazilian rhythms. My head became light and dizzy. I was reclining on the sofa. Alain slipped a hand behind my waist and carried me to the bedroom, which was bare with white walls, except for a large mattress on the floor with sheets and blankets. He undressed me slowly. I was numb and suddenly things appeared to move in slow motion. Alain made love to me a number of times. His virility was stupendous. Both of us perspiring profusely, and he dried me gently with the sheets. We slept in each other's arms.

The next morning, I found a note on the floor near the mattress, telling me to stay in bed. Alain came from the kitchen, waist wrapped with a towel, muscles tan and taut, holding a tray with two cups of strong, fragrant coffee, flaky croissants, and boiled eggs. I was famished! While eating, I told him that he was a fantastic lover. He smiled enigmatically. I had wanted to hear words of endearments, but he just started to dress, so I got up, went to the bathroom to shower and dress.

The next two days were like a dream. Dinners in dimly lit bistros and nights of passionate lovemaking. Drained and emptied, the last day found me in a little park, sitting on a bench, incapable of moving and aching all over. I was numb on the outside but filled inside with indescribable ecstasy. I had been fulfilled physically, but what about heart and soul? That night during lovemaking, Alain broke his reserve and said, "Je t'aime, Je t'aime." At the airport, it was a sad goodbye. I was falling in love with love and romance.

Two days after my arrival home, I was awakened by Alain's voice on the telephone. "Je t'aime." Then I heard the Brazilian music in the background. We talked, it seemed, for hours; it was wonderful. A month later, I was back in Paris. At the airport, I found a smiling Alain with bouquets of red roses in each hand, waving wildly at me from the arrival gate. In the apartment, he had written on all the windows and mirrors, "Je t'aime. Bienvenue." There were vases of red roses everywhere. It was touching. That first week it was ecstasy all over again: cozy dinners followed by lovemaking nights of passion. The mattress was still on the floor!

I returned to the little square on the same bench; the leaves were turning red. I was reflecting on this idyll. I was indulging from life all the juices of love, but somehow a little voice in the back of my mind was giving me warning signals. Alain would leave for work. His office was in a plush building on the Champs Elysées. He was working in public relations for a renowned jewelry firm. Early mornings he would dress fastidiously, gulp a cup of espresso, and disappear until late evening. One day, as I was looking for something in the living room, under a small round table covered with a red plaid cloth, I saw a box. My curiosity got the best of me. I opened it and saw some black silk scarfs, a miniature tool box and, to my horror, a long stiletto knife and a pair of black gloves. I closed the box quickly. My heart was pounding fast and a wave of fear swept over me. Could it be? Alain, a dangerous thief? And the knife? Maybe I was just letting my imagination get the best of me.

I was trying to remain calm as evening came. Alain had made reservations for us to dine at La Cascade, a restaurant in the Bois de Boulogne. I was wearing my red silk dress with my dark hair in a smart chignon, and Alain was in a white suit. We made a grand entrance. I was still uneasy, but determined not to ask questions. During dinner, he inquired about my activities for the next day. I told him that I made plans to view an art auction with my friend Lyvia. He left the table twice to make telephone calls. He paid the check and we drove at a maddening speed back to the apartment.

It was eleven o'clock and he said that he would be back in an hour. I pressed him for answers, but he pushed me aside and abruptly left. In a state of nervousness and fear, I paced the room. Where would he go at this time of night? To what sinister rendezvous? My mind was in chaos. No! I must not get worried. Alain is a gentleman; he will return soon. To calm myself, I undressed and took a long hot bath, lingering in the tub. Placing some Brazilian tapes on the stereo, I was slowly regaining my composure. Sipping hot tea, looking at the clock, now half past two, I could not sleep. Every fifteen minutes I glanced at my watch. Maybe he went to see another woman. That I thought I could deal with, but why have me stay with him these past two weeks? I was exhausted from speculating. Around five o'clock in the morning, I finally fell asleep.

I awoke sharply, hearing a key in the door. It was eight by my wristwatch. Alain appeared with clothes rumpled, hair mussed, and a faint odor of whiskey about him. He undressed and, without a word, collapsed on the mattress and went to sleep. That day we had our first quarrel. I told him that I needed a vacation and that I was going to a little village in the Alps for a few days to rest. He made no comment and was almost cold. I did not question him about where he had gone the night before. We were lovers and our bonds were purely physical though I had hoped for something more.

Once in our intimate talks, Alain had told me that he was an only child, raised by a single, military-minded father. As a very young man, he had gone to India to follow a guru and traveled extensively in that country. Among his qualities was an almost feminine sensitivity. But he also possessed steely gray piercing eyes. My need to get away left him noncommittal. While taking only a small overnight bag and a camera, I placed my other suitcase and a large bag in the closet, where I had stashed some extra traveler's checks.

Alain drove me to the train station and I was en route for St. Jean, a small village in the French Valais region, with flowers on windowsills of picturesque wooden houses. Cows in the verdant prairies, lazily grazed the lush grass, tinkling bells around their necks. I found a charming inn and settled in a tiny room smelling of pine. The small bed was covered with a thick down blanket. Windows opened on the fragrant valley below, so very peaceful and quiet. Here I could restore my body and take stock of my feelings for Alain.

Four days passed quickly, with long walks, hearty food and sound sleep to awaken by the tinkling of the cow bells. St. Jean, a tiny hamlet in the French Valais, was typical of the region. A small group of people gathered near shady doorways, dressed in colorful costumes. Women in large skirts and pretty embroidered aprons, men in leather pants, singing and yodeling in the crisp mountain air. I took their pictures, framed by red geraniums and the clear blue sky. I also painted a dozen watercolors of green valleys and narrow lanes, houses decorated with flowers, water mills near brooks, and the snow-capped Alps.

When I returned to Paris, I had gained a few pounds and my cheeks were rosy. Alain was in a good mood. I was tired after a long train ride so I went to bed early. The next morning, while going through my clothes in the bag that I had not taken to St. Jean, I found that half of my traveler's checks were missing, some seven hundred dollars. I got panicky and recounted several times what was left, always with the same results. I tried to recall my possibly misplacing that sum, but to no avail. It was gone. Could Alain have taken it? I will never know.

I left Paris two days later, pretending there was an emergency at home. Alain never called me again. The following winter I was back in Paris. A year had passed and I saw my friend Lyvia, who was now dabbling in the occult. She told me that Alain had been arrested and sent to prison on grand theft charges. A ten million dollar burglary had occurred in the jewelry firm where he worked. It had made big headlines in the French newspapers. But Lyvia was so strange now that I did not know if and when to believe her. She was even adept at black magic. I had a sensation of disenchantment, a train of sadness, and feelings of sorrow.

I was still living in my cozy apartment in Palo Alto with Gregg, who was going to the University in San Francisco. One day, when he was nineteen years old, Gregg announced that he was going on a trip to Mexico with a young friend from school whose family had a place there and had invited him. I was curious and wanted to meet the mother of the friend and ask some questions. It was arranged and Lupe came to my place. I had set a table with tea and pastries. We chatted. She professed admiration and affection for my son. So both young men left for Mexico and had a great trip. As soon as Gregg called, my fears were gone.

Several weeks went by when Lupe called me to invite me to visit her where she worked. She was a housekeeper, trying to help her large family of five children and husband. She worked for an elderly gentleman, a widower. We drove to a residential part of town up on a hill, to a beautiful, colonial-style mansion. We entered through an impressive foyer with a marble staircase leading to various rooms, including a sunny living room filled with antiques and objects d'art.

Sitting by the window was a silver-haired, slender man with smiling blue eyes. Lupe introduced him as Carl Otto Baum. As I started to shake hands, Mr. Baum put his arms around me and smiled. I was very surprised at that. We had tea that Lupe had prepared. I admired the house, I commented on the lovely Persian carpets, the Georgian silver candelabra, the Oriental Coromandel screens, and the Persian miniatures. Carl, as he wanted me to call him, had traveled extensively all his life. We had things in common, and the visit was friendly. Carl asked for my telephone number and the next day he called me to have lunch with him. We chose a lovely restaurant for this occasion and I enjoyed the meal and his company.

The next few weeks were busy at the studio, but I managed to have several more lunches with Carl. He had passed retirement age and was in demand as a consultant for big industrial companies and worked with many international conglomerates. For the next few months, we saw each other frequently and I developed a great affection for this shy distinguished gentleman. Carl was absolutely smitten with me and would call me every day. Gregg was happy for me, as he had met Carl on several occasions, doing gardening work on the estate.

Dancer of Bali
and woodcarver of UBUD

my second trip To
Bali on my
Honeymoon with Karl
1981

One day, I received a call from the Prudential Cruise line. I was scheduled to leave on what was to be my last cruise with the company, a two-month trip around South America. Carl was sad and I promised to write often. The trip was excellent, my work was greatly appreciated, and I had a lot of time to think about Carl. I knew that sometime in the future I would either terminate the friendship or marry him. The age difference was considerable, he being thirty years my senior. But, on the plus side he had a great sense of humor, a brilliant mind, and a strong constitution. I would have to give up lovers. Oh, but to have the security of a home that had eluded me all my life. Gregg would be so happy for me to be settled, a married woman. I could pursue ardently my artistic career. It was tantalizing and I could dream of living in the mansion.

Upon my return, I explained to Carl that I would have to go away on trips from time to time, to get inspiration, my gypsy soul eager to take flight. Carl proposed, and I accepted. We had a most wonderful engagement party at the mansion. Carl told me that he missed me so much that he wanted me with him all the time. We talked about a honeymoon and revisiting the places that we both knew. Our wedding was a simple ceremony, with only the immediate families and witnesses present. My darling friend Bianca was my witness. I had redecorated the bedroom and put large mirrors on the wardrobe. That first night when we slept on the huge four-poster bed with a canopy. As I looked in the mirror, I could not help but say to my reflection, "You are now the mistress of the house. How truly wonderful, how truly exciting."

I settled in as a married woman that year after a wondrous honeymoon that took us to Tokyo, Hong Kong, Bali, Bangkok, and Honolulu. Carl was attentive and generous, buying me a lovely ruby in Thailand. I shopped extensively in Hong Kong for clothes. How truly luxurious life was. Staying in plush hotels like the Oriental in Bangkok, the Okura in Tokyo. At the Peninsula in Hong Kong, a uniformed valet was at our beck and call. After shopping, we would find a steaming teapot accompanied by sweets awaiting us in our suite.

I sensed that Carl needed to have a project, as most of his life he had been quite active. I had always dreamed of having a large studio with enormous glass windows and skylights. It was my cherished dream to be able to paint on a large scale. So Carl, with the aid of an architect and some carpenters, created a large wooden structure at the far corner of the garden, complete with windows from ceiling to floor, with skylights, where sun and light flooded the entire inside. The project included a gazebo with a Japanese wooden hot tub. Lovely exotic plants surrounded my studio. A flagstone terrace united the studio to the back of the house, where there was a solarium full of plants and a state-of-the-art kitchen.

I was happy! Between cooking meals of delicious Oriental cuisine and painting, it was my fantasy world come true. But things were peaceful only on the surface. At times I felt as if I was in a glass bowl. Carl was sweet and I was affectionate with him, sitting on his lap after dinner, hugging him and caressing his cheeks, which had fine wrinkles. The blue of his eyes and the snow white hair melted my heart and I would whisper words of endearment to him.

That first year was very productive. I had a routine, and painted in the morning after a long walk. We would get our breakfasts separately as Carl was up early working in the garden. He loved flowers and would be forever planting and puttering in the tool shed. After my walk, I would shower and go to the studio and paint, interrupted often by telephone calls or cooking. Even so, I did produce a large quantity of paintings.

As summer came, my soul was restless. I often would dream of the countryside of Provence and of the lovely sites painted by the Impressionists. The art books that Carl bought me only frustrated me. They were so beautifully illustrated with the works of Monet, Cezanne, and Renoir. I was longing to paint in the lavender and poppy fields. One evening at dinner, I talked about France and travel. I told Carl that I was running dry of subjects to paint and needed inspiration. After much cajoling on my part, with promises to have an art exhibit in France to generate more income, Carl came around. If my arguments were valid, Carl could be swayed. We decided to take a trip to France. It was to be for two reasons: to meet some relatives in England and France, and to find a place to paint and spend at least six months in the south of France. My desire was to find a house and paint in the surrounding hills of Provence and to have an art exhibit.

We left on a chilly March day and flew to Paris. After settling into our luxurious Hotel George V, we went to dinner and slept a long time because of jet lag. We called my brother Andy and his wife to say that we had arrived safely. We visited some distant relatives and took them to dinner at Le Fouquet. I have always loved that restaurant on the Champs Elysées. This marriage will work, I said to myself. If only we can find a decent house to rent in the South of France. That week in Paris, I shopped at the Galerie Lafayette for clothes and luggage. I intended to bring lots of gifts back home. I was thrilled to smell the fragrant mimosa again as we arrived in Nice. We settled at the plush Hotel Negresco. After a few weeks of exhausting days with our scouring the countryside above Nice and Cannes, we found, near an old chateau, a lovely pink villa, complete with flowering bougainvillaea on the balcony and a large flagstone terrace. It had several large sunny rooms on two floors, a tiny but functional kitchen, and a large living room with a mantel and a big fireplace. The view was lovely; we could see the Alps with snowcaps. A smell of lavender permeated the air. I fell in love with that place. The villa was one of about twenty houses surrounded by olive trees. There were lots of lawns and stone terraces, and a large pool. On top of the hill was a chateau. I had to do a lot of cajoling with Carl, as he was reluctant at first to rent this place. But I promised to work hard and sell my paintings to pay for expenses.

We moved in and it was wonderful. I felt so good. The air was exhilarating and my energy was high. Those six months were the best of my life. We would go to Cannes, eat in the little restaurants I had known in my youth. We attended the glamorous film festival in May. We traveled and I painted. On one occasion, Carl and I visited a Holocaust survivor, a writer. Martin Gray and his wife lived in a house on a hill above Cannes. Martin, a small man with gray hair, had lost one eye in the Warsaw Ghetto and somehow survived. He was only a young boy in those days of horror. Later, after he married, he and his wife had four children. But Martin lost his first wife and all their children in Luberon to a forest fire. The miracle was that he could start again. He remarried and when we visited him we met his new wife and their three children. During those six months, we visited an art exhibit at Hotel Montfleury in Cannes. This show is what influenced me to exhibit my paintings in the south of France in the next years, from 1981 to 1990.

On our first stay at the villa, we had relatives visit us; on one occasion, Andy and Ingrid with their two daughters, Anya and Marusha. It was good to see them. They had made their home in France. Carl had some bad spells and was becoming irritable. We also had a visit from Gregg, who stayed with us. My son drove with us from Monaco to Lago Como and Milano and into Geneva, stopping en route in Saint Tropez. We stayed overnight at the Hotel Byblos to enjoy the warm weather. We went to La Colombe d'Or, a favorite haunt of Simone Signoret and Yves Montand. We lunched on the terrace overlooking the verdant hills and I reminisced of my first romance long ago, here in the same place.

Gregg had to return home to his studies and we stayed on for our last month before returning to our house in California, where it was summer. I had a renewed enthusiasm as I had secured a contract to exhibit in Nice in a major hotel. We returned home, I with a strong inspiration to paint and with many photos of lush fields of roses that bloomed behind our villa and of lavender fields. We were not far from Grasse, where flowers were grown for the town's perfumeries. I still had in my mind the pink village of Mougins: the cobblestones, the narrow lane of Vence and the flower market, the sky's vivid hue, the swaying palm trees. With a vengeance, I set out to work in my new studio with its high skylight. I painted every day that year. My goal was to ship about fifty canvasses to Nice by the following spring. Carl was happy to be home again. Nothing had changed. The house was lovely. We had Rosa to look after the cleaning, as Lupe had left us, and our gardener to care for the grounds. Gregg would visit often and have dinner with us. My most relaxing time was in the hot tub. Carl and I had no sex life, but we were very affectionate to one another. Often he would give me a massage. He had good, nurturing hands. If I would have lunch with a girl friend, or if Bianca visited me, Carl and I would wind up in a bitter argument. He was jealous of my friendships.

That winter, near the holidays, we decided to spend a week in Honolulu. We flew in a cold December to Hawaii. It was so wonderful to see the white powdered sand of the Royal Hawaiian Hotel. The Christmas holiday crowd was there. We had seven leisurely days that went by too fast, then back to the house and paintings with occasional trips to San Francisco. I lured Carl to the opera one night before the end of the season. He looked nice in his black tuxedo.

In March of 1984, we returned to France to the villa in preparation for my exhibit at the Hotel Regency in Nice. It was to be the first of three exhibits in Nice in the following years. I had also secured a contract to hold a show in Deauville, Normandy in July. We had to call the ship chandler in Marseilles as my shipment of paintings had been delayed. I was a nervous wreck. I had shipped many paintings, not all framed, just stretched. I was busy getting paintings framed by a store in Nice. The first show was to be in June in Nice for three weeks. The next show was to be in Deauville in July for the whole month. I worked frantically. Carl was reading on the terrace most of the time, but we had words often. I thought he was not feeling in his element and was often frustrated not being able to understand the language. He missed his home, his garden, and his cronies.

After a couple of months, Carl returned home, leaving me with my exhibits. I managed quite well. Not wanting to return to the villa upon the hill late at night, I rented a room in the Hotel Regency for the time of the exhibit. The obliging manager gave me a preferred rate and I had a lovely room. The show was a success. At the Regency I had had reviews in the press and many people came to the vernissage. It was good for the hotel to have an artist exhibit. I had a large space in the hall and lots of help to hang my paintings. The sales were brisk and some collectors would buy more than one work.

That year, many Arabs from the Emirate were visiting Cannes and Nice. They lounged in their white garb, mingling with the French and the international crowd of sunbathers in sandals. In the evenings they socialized with the glamorous young French vacationers. I was at my little desk from early in the morning until midnight every day, with only an occasional trip to my room to await Carl's call. He telephoned me every day. Some evenings, if business was slow, I would go to the bar and flirt with the bartender. The employees of the hotel began to treat me as one of them. I gave each one a brochure and a signed poster. At the end my three-week show I had sold many paintings and my guest book was filled with names and addresses of the buyers.

I had only a few days to collect the other paintings I had saved for the show in Deauville at the Hotel Normandy. I was to stay for a month there. I sent the paintings in wooden crates and took the train to Deauville. I remember the verdant plateau and the lush greenery with fat cattle in the pasture of the Norman landscape, the hot wind through the window of my train compartment. I had packed a suitcase with elegant outfits and dresses, as Deauville in season is quite elegant, with horse racing and Parisian jet-setters!

Arriving at the hotel, I was met by the charming director, Hans. He was a Dutchman and extremely well groomed and courteous. I was shown the display area. It was smaller than I had expected, but I could manage to exhibit about thirty to forty paintings. It was an area with a mezzanine where the reception was to be held. I was pleasantly surprised at the number of people attending the opening party. My brother Andy came and I was happy to see him. The paintings, with the warm colors of the south of France, attracted a large crowd.

The Hotel Normandy had been built at the turn of the century. Its outdoor restaurant exuded charm, as did the old gabled buildings of the waterfront near the casino. It was elegant with its lovely chandelier and gambling rooms. The area attracted a coterie of international travelers and tourists from nearby Paris. Sales of my paintings started slowly, but I was patient. I took an occasional walk on the beach with its wooden pier. It was very crowded. As usual, I took photographs for future reference.

One evening as I was returning to my room, Hans invited me to his suite for a glass of sherry. We chatted. He was very attentive and gallant. After a couple of drinks, as I was leaving, he took me in his arms and we kissed. It was so unexpected, but I knew that I missed the attentions of a younger man. Carl was not calling me every week and it was very difficult to be faithful. The next night, the inevitable happened. Hans made sweet love to me. He was married also, but his wife was in Paris. We were both lonely and it was a long hot month of July. I did not feel guilty; my body did crave. I was more in tune with the rest of the world.

Eventually the exhibit went well. I returned to the villa and made preparations to fly home to San Francisco. When I saw Carl, he looked frail, but happy to see me. I was elated with the success of my exhibits and related all to Carl, except, of course, my infidelity. I vowed to make it up to him and was kind, paying him lots of attention, cooking meals, and at every chance being affectionate.

We spent the Christmas vacation in Kauai. It was lovely to be in Hawaii again that winter of 1985. The warm breeze, the lovely room by the lagoon, the coco palms, and every evening cocktails and dinner with charming guests of the hotel. The few days passed quickly.

Returning home, I worked diligently as I had secured a month-long contract to exhibit at the prestigious Hotel de Paris in Monaco in July 1986. Not only at the height of the season, but also at the time when Princess Grace was to be the honorary chairwoman of the Red Cross Gala. I painted every day, morning until dark.

That winter, a roaring fire in our fireplace and a little music were my only relaxation in the evenings. Carl would retire to his study and then to his bedroom. Our relationship was a bit strained around the subject of finances. I had to assume all the expenses of shipping my paintings to France plus the airfare and reservations at the Hotel de Paris, where I was to stay. Carl was jealous, although proud, of my achievements. He was also irritated and annoyed that I had to go for even the few months of the exhibits. The atmosphere was tense at home. I confided my feelings to my close friend Bianca. She was very helpful, if only in listening to me.

I prepared a collection of sixty paintings by May. Carl was busy building crates to ship them. When he worked with his hands, he seemed happy. Everything was ready and the transport company came to fetch the big crates. It was to take two months by sea to Marseilles and then to Monaco by truck.

Gregg, who was now on his own, had met a lovely young woman. While

I was in France, they were engaged to be married. After I returned, their wedding was held in a lovely old mansion in San Francisco. Two hundred guests attended, including our little family of grandparents. An emotional Miles hugged me. He was so proud of Gregg! Carl and I were proud, too. The bride and groom looked so ravishing. It was one of the happiest times of my life. For their honeymoon, Kitt and Gregg were going to be in the south of France to attend my first big exhibit in Monaco.

I left with high anticipation of an exciting summer in Monte Carlo. I settled into a small hotel near the prestigious Hotel de Paris as I could not afford the high rate in full season. The manager of the Hotel de Paris gave me carte blanche and lots of help from the bellboys and hotel staff to hang my paintings. Everyone was courteous and kind and professed admiration for my work. I had the beautiful Salon Beaumarchais to myself. On a large table was a bouquet of gorgeous fresh flowers sent to me by some friends. I displayed posters and brochures. I had walked the streets of Monte Carlo to place the posters, which were printed with one of my paintings, in various stores, perfumeries, libraries, restaurants, and hotels.

The big day of the vernissage came and it was extremely successful with the large crowd in attendance. Gregg and Kitt arrived. She looked lovely in a long summer white dress. A smiling Gregg was handsome in a light gray suit and red tie. Andy was there with his older daughter, Marusha. Everyone had gorgeous tans and, of course, we took lots of photos. I wore a green dress with confetti dots to accentuate my cleavage and deep tan. My long dark hair was smartly coiffed. The vernissage ended and I had made some sales, which was unusual as people tended to be occupied with each other rather than look at paintings. The theme of the exhibit was "Belle Epoque." Renoir and Monet were my main influences. The show had a good opening. An article appeared in the Monte Carlo paper the next day with favorable comments.

I was happy, spending time with my son, his wife, and my brother Andy, who had to leave for home after only a few days. I remained the month of July and sold many paintings. Each night I awaited Carl's telephone call and related to him all the activities and progress of the exhibit. I would also receive mail from Carl, endearing letters. I felt that I was accomplishing something when all day long I received compliments from clients and collectors for my paintings. I was extremely pleased that all my efforts were appreciated.

At night in the small hotel room, I counted the money from my sales and deposited the bills in an envelope for the bank. The rent for the salon was paid in advance by me. I felt that Carl withdrew financial help for my exhibits as a way of getting back at me for being away from him. But soon, I would be returning to a lovely home and otherwise loving husband. The situation of our relationship suited me. That summer I was even able to put money aside, thanks to the volume of sales of my paintings. This was something I had never been able to do before. Yet something was still missing in my satisfaction. My life didn't seem fulfilled.

Many celebrities stopped by the salon to view my exhibit and sign the guest book. Prince Albert of Monaco, titled ladies, and movie stars entered their names in my gold book and added supportive comments. Women with lovely evening dresses and their escorts would stop by after dinner to view my paintings and gamble at the casino. One of my largest and most ambitious paintings entitled "Pigeon Feeding in Monaco" attracted a lot of attention. It had lovely shades of pastel colors in pinks and oranges. One afternoon a young German couple came and was so taken by the painting that they came the next day with thousands of francs in cash and bought it. That was the most expensive painting that I had sold so far.

I would often go to the other hotels in Monaco for a change of atmosphere and to listen to music. I would spend time at the Loew's Hotel as it was more like an American hotel. I was comfortable in the lounge where I listened to piano music. The month was over and I was to return home after a short stop in Paris. I met a charming young Frenchman by the name of Daniel. For three days we had a romance and made love. Daniel was a skilled lover and I knew then how much I had missed physical contact the past few years. Guilt did not enter my mind as Carl could not satisfy me and I was in my prime time of sexual desire. I wanted to be with Daniel longer, but I had to return home. We promised to write and to see each other in a few months.

It was raining when I arrived home to a smiling Carl. But his back was stooping more and I felt a tinge of pity. I did love him in my own way and was more affectionate than ever, making lovely candle-lit dinners every evening. That winter, we took a trip to Mexico. Carl wanted to see the pyramids of Uxmal and Chichén Itza. It was a grueling, tiring trip. In retrospect, I do not think we should have undertaken it in view of Carl's fragility and age. Carl took sick upon our return but recovered amazingly fast.

I painted more than ever in the winter of 1986. In the following spring, with a new collection and the salon's rent paid, I returned to Monte Carlo to prepare for an exhibit. I had rented a small apartment near the hotel for the months of May, June, and July. One weekend that summer, my friend Lisa and I took an excursion bus to Venice. It was wonderful to see that city. Upon our return to Monte Carlo, a telegram was delivered. Carl had succumbed to a heart attack. I was devastated. I met Andy in Paris and we flew home for the funeral.

Chapter Seven

IN THE FALL OF 1988 I returned to Italy and saw the Amalfi coast, which I had missed on previous visits. My objective was to spend a week in Capri to paint and revisit this lovely island which I had known in my young years as a student. After staying a few days with friends in Monte Carlo and Menton, I took the train for Rome. I wanted to spend a day in the Eternal City as I had not been there for a good number of years.

I traveled light, in jeans, with a small suitcase and a bag attached to a caddy. The train trip was uneventful! Roma Termini was large and very crowded. Nearby I saw the sign for Tivoli Albergo. I went in and secured a room for the night. The weather was warm and after resting for a few hours, I went to see the Coliseum. In the bright noon sun it looked beautiful and timeless. I took lots of photos and then walked around the ancient city. I took a bus to Vatican City. Entering the old arches to the huge St. Peter's Place, lined with souvenir vendors, I admired the splendid setting complete with statuary. After entering the Vatican I went to see the Pieta of Michelangelo, which was now protected by a glass wall. In the dim light the sorrowful marble statue of "The descent from the Cross" gleamed palely. I walked through the gates to the city of Rome, and left the Vatican behind.

The balmy September weather was pleasant. I ambled down Via Veneto, which looked peaceful and provincial, but with no more horse-drawn carriages. Many sidewalk cafés were closed. The terraces had an air of abandonment and sadness. A feeling of times past made me long to be in Capri. To get a good night's rest I hastened to my hotel.

The next morning, I took a relatively short train ride to Napoli. After consulting with several train officials, speaking in halting Italian, I found that I should get off the train before the stop in Napoli. Just a short walk from the station found me at the pier for the boats to Capri. I arrived there as a fast boat was preparing to pull out. Hurriedly, I purchased my ticket and embarked with fifty other passengers who were mostly Neapolitans. The weather was hot and humid, in late summer, and the people wore their best apparel.

After a short ride, the boat pulled into the Bay of Capri. The docks were crowded with small crafts and a cruise liner, the Motoscaffi, and hydrofoil ferries. I found the scene familiar, with the bay surrounded by jagged mountains. Walking by the funicular that ascended directly to the piazzetta, I continued along the quais. On the hill that bordered the sea, I admired the view and took in deep breaths of the fragrant sea air. The road started to climb as I pulled my luggage behind me.

In the distance I saw a sign that read, "Albergo del Mare." I went in. The prices had staggeringly increased since my last visit years ago. I rested in the small dark room with closed shutters. Later on, I ventured to the docks in search of a trattoria for dinner. I was exhausted when I returned to the hotel for a night's rest. I slept poorly, bothered by mosquitoes. When morning came I was glad to leave.

Once more I started to climb the steep hill and pulled my luggage behind me. In the early morning, I saw in the distance a small orange bus chugging up the hill. It was the local island transportation for the workers going to Anacapri. When the bus stopped, I got in. The sleepy Capriots made room for me and my suitcase. When we arrived at the Piazzetta, I got out. The sky was very blue, the mountains tinted with a green hue. I found myself in the small square with the baroque Byzantine church and the spectacular view of the sea surrounded by tall jagged mountains. White columns graced with purple bougainvillaeas stood near the entrance of the funicular, the Piazzetta was quiet in the early morning. A few cafés were open, but the terraces were deserted. I spotted a café worker setting up tables and chairs. I went in and ordered a steaming cup of cappuccino with thick foam. I felt good, elated.

A short, slightly balding man was sweeping the café floor. I asked him if he knew of a hotel or pension. He recommended the Pension Felice and gave me the complicated directions. I speculated that it was much too far and hard to find. But I decided to investigate and strolled again past the Piazzetta. After missing many turns, I finally found my way. Pension Felice was a half-finished stone hodge-podge of a house of whitewashed stucco. As I approached the entryway, down a few steps, I noticed its neglected garden and burned lemon trees. The view was blocked by thick bushes. A man was in the entrance hall, his dark hair greasy and unkempt, his shirt opened. I asked him for the price of a room. He mumbled something in Italian. I thanked him politely but hurriedly left, glad to get out of there.

I returned to the Piazzetta, which was getting crowded now with tourists arriving on the day's first ferry from Naples. I walked past the cafés again, still searching for a hotel. Sandwiched between the souvenir shops, restaurants and café terraces, I saw a minuscule hotel, "Blue Mare." I climbed the one flight of stairs up to it.

So tired by now, I came upon a bourgeois living room, complete with couch, chairs, television, paintings on the wall and a small desk to the left of the entrance. An old, stout woman with white hair and dressed in black sat by the window. Another elderly woman was on her knees scrubbing the floor. A younger woman came from the back, which I presumed was the kitchen. When I asked for a room, she took a quick look at me and responded affirmatively. When I asked the price, it was astronomically high in liras, converting to fifty dollars a night. I explained that I was an artist on a budget and might stay a week. We agreed on forty dollars a night. I did not wish to go any further. The place looked clean enough.

The small room she showed me was immaculate. It had two beds, an armoire and a sink. She explained to me that the communal bathroom was across the hall. The windows of my room opened to a sweeping view of the sea and mountains. She gave me the key and I unpacked a few things. My canvases, watercolors, paints and brushes were placed neatly in the armoire along with my clothes. I opened the windows to let air in. The price had been high but it was still tourist season and, at any rate, I had been fortunate to find this hotel so convenient to the Piazzetta and with a view. The only drawback was the constant noise below, as trucks full of vegetables and fruits discharged their cargo.

Putting on comfortable shoes and taking my sketchpad, I walked out of the room. The woman at the desk asked me for my passport and had me register. She then gave me a card that read "Blue Mare, F. Cremolini, Director." I sauntered to the Piazzetta, endeavoring to do some sketching, first of the church and the clock with its Moorish silhouette. I found a perfect vantage point, the first floor of the tea room facing the church. After another cup of coffee, I asked the waiter if I could sit at a small table on the top floor balcony overlooking the Piazzetta. Since it was not yet teatime, the place was quiet. The young Italian waiters and waitresses smiled and told me to make myself comfortable to paint. I did some excellent sketches in pen and ink for about two hours. I then left.

Feeling hungry, I stopped at a nearby trattoria for a delicious pizza. Thus restored, I ambled back to the Piazzetta, past the many elegant shops, boutiques, and curio shops. How different from those past years when the island had only a few small shops. The tourist trade ruled Capri now. I wanted to rediscover the Capri of my youth and clung to the hope that it still existed. Perhaps I would find my Capri in the Marina Piccola with the Farraglioni and the fishermen with their gaily-colored boats. Or perhaps in Marina Grande at the Canzone del Mare, or in the beautiful resort of Grace Field. But there were no more small donkeys, laden with baskets filled with fruit and flowers, trodding along the Via del Mare. No more soulful-eyed guitarists singing their greetings as you disembarked from your boat at the docks. That was another era.

I returned to the hotel in mid-afternoon. At the desk there was a man smiling a toothy grin through a thick mustache. I asked him for my passport, which he handed me promptly. He spoke English haltingly, so after a while we chatted in French, which he spoke with a charming Italian accent. He was Signor Flavio Cremolini, the director or patrone. His daughter was the woman who had greeted me and his wife the older woman who scrubbed the floors. Obviously the old lady was the Mamma.

I went to my room to freshen up and change my clothes. It was still light and I could work for another hour. Returning to the Piazzetta with more sketch paper, I was inspired. It was, by now, five o'clock. The sky was still a vivid blue. Walking past grocery stores, I decided to buy some fruits and delicious Italian bread with cheese and proscuitto to eat in my room. Later, laden with fragrantly ripe grapes the color of wine and a few juicy pears, I returned to the hotel to drop off my brown bag of dinner.

Once more I was out, skipping on the cobblestones, exploring the alleyways, looking for the right spot to paint. The whitewashed walls with splashes of deep vibrant red bougainvillaeas, the orange roofs, the arches with the clinging vines, on the horizon the blue sea, the vibrant iridescent sky. After six o'clock, when the shadows were more pronounced and turned purple gray, was the best time for me to put colors on my palette to paint. The whitewashed wall tinted indigo by the fading light. I worked fast, putting light touches on the paper. It began to look like a soft scene in a mist. At another spot I painted a balcony with flowers hanging, stairs, alleys, a cat sleeping in a doorway, and always the deep cerulean sky above. Many sketches later, I returned to the hotel and unloaded my work.

The next two days I did the same, and each time I found Signor Cremolini smiling his greeting to me. His daughter however, always showed a sour face. His wife, perpetually scrubbing the floors, ignored me totally. Sometimes, in the evenings upon coming back, I would find them sitting in the living room eating from steamy plates of pasta at the small table, watching a blaring television. Some wonderful smell wafted from the kitchen and Signor Flavio would come and dish out of the frying pan some steamy orange-yellow peppers onto their tomato-sauced pasta dish. It looked so cozy and normal. This family style was in such contrast to the bustling Capri of the tourists only a few feet away. I was the only resident in the small hotel. Two rooms on the first floor and two rooms upstairs were vacant. A tiny alcove near the entrance was for the "Nonna" and next to it was the owner's bedroom, the "Camera de Letto Matrimoniale."

I was inspired! So the next day I decided to paint a scene at the docks. Early on my third day in Capri, after a frugal breakfast of rolls and strong coffee and armed with my canvas, my tubes of paints and my brushes, I set off for the docks. On this glorious sunny and warm day of September, I did my usual walk down the cobblestones of the Via del Mare, soon arriving by the dock area. The ferries of the Caremar fleet were disgorging their passengers for the day.

Looking for just the right spot, I walked past restaurants and souvenir shops near the water's edge. A flotilla of small gaily-colored boats and fishing vessels would do nicely for the foreground but I needed a dramatic touch for the background. As I passed a gas pump near a fishing boat, I saw it. Below the jagged hills with their verdant green foliage and small cubist houses, the waterfront came alive with its buildings the color of rust, pale orange, pinks, and soft yellows. I selected a small portion of the view.

I was exhilarated. Nothing compared to the feeling of having a perfect day and a sublime view to paint. I spotted an old fisherman's bench and a rickety chair served as my easel. Squeezed from their tubes, my paints in lush colors spread on my palette. Soon I was absorbed with my work. My head was protected by a visored cap. The sun was on my back. It was a glorious, almost sensual feeling to paint outdoors, "en plein air." I was at peace with myself, and with a few strokes, I put everything in place.

And soon, the painting took on its own life, colors bursting, sinuous shapes, curving lines, bold strokes. As I painted, I smiled with happiness. After awhile, I got up to view my work at a distance. As I painted some more, I sensed a presence behind my back. I turned around and saw two rugged, sunburned fishermen looking curiously at my painting. I explained in Italian to them that it was not finished. They grinned and walked away. My painting was coming along very well, the foreground with the aquamarine bold strokes, the small curved shapes of the fishing boats in the background were lined in a semi-circle of bold colors.

I started another canvas and turned slightly to get a different view. The spot was fantastic. I could have done four or five scenes, but the time passed quickly and the sun was slowly departing from the sky. I started to clean my brushes and scrape my palette. As I walked away, the two fishermen came around and asked to see my paintings. I showed them and they said, "Bene, Bene." I replied, "No e finito." My critics smiled again and I said, "Domani ritorna," as I intended to return the next day.

It was bright and sunny the next morning as I returned to finish my work and found the now familiar bench. After an hour or so, I was satisfied with the look of my paintings. I held the canvases at arm's length to let them dry and walked the docks, looking for a trattoria to have lunch. A man in a white apron stood by a restaurant and smiled at me and tried to get a glimpse of my paintings. Sensing his curiosity, I turned the canvas around to show him. He admired my work and gave me compliments. We engaged in conversation. I showed him more sketches. He was impressed and invited me to enter his restaurant for a cup of coffee. I confided to him that my visit to Capri was nostalgic. I had been there in my youth. The man was attentive and very appreciative of art.

As the noon hour approached, he excused himself to wait on the customers who had started to arrive. I sat there and, having another waterfront view, I started to sketch. Sitting on the terrace, I saw people coming in. An older man, followed by a younger one, both dressed in yachting clothes, entered and sat nearby. The owner came and greeted them profusely. He sat and talked to the two men at great length, describing the menu and the catch of the day, which he brought to the table. They were, without a doubt, good clients and friends. While they ate, they glanced in my direction. After a short while, the younger man came by my table to see my work. I gave him some sketches to show his friend, who was now drinking his cup of espresso. They invited me to join them for my second cup of espresso. My spirits were high as I proudly showed my watercolor scenes and took the compliments modestly. After the presentation, Count Maximillan Camogli was on his yacht for a fortnight. In the ensuing conversation I suggested to do a painting of his yacht. I was invited the next morning for a visit and was given directions. After a last "ciao," I left the restaurant.

The rest of the day passed agreeably, sketching the rocks and beach of Marina Piccola: the arch of the rock formation, the aqua color of the translucent water, the rainbow colored fishing boats. I took many photos as I stood at the edge of the water and later as I walked the steps to Grace Field Canzona del Mare. It was mostly deserted with an air of desolation, where once was the hub of Capri.

I took the little orange bus back to the Piazzetta. To see the Farraglioni at sunset was my objective so I walked the lovely path to the gardens. As I paused a brief moment by the wall, I saw Flavio, the owner of the hotel, holding a handkerchief to his nose. We greeted each other. Walking side by side, he confessed he was suffering from hay fever during his promenade of the day. He offered to stop for a coffee. The tearoom was cool inside. After the heat of the day, it felt good, as we sat at a small table.

Signor Flavio was a great talker and confided in me that his marriage was a terrible burden and constant humiliation as his wife was twenty years older than he. In intimate confidence, he shared with me that sleeping in his matrimonial bed was a torture every night. He suffered greatly in this situation. His soul was romantic and poetic. Also, he let me know that he was terribly attracted to me. I was surprised and, I must say, a little flattered. I told him that my stay would end in four days and that I still had to see Amalfi, Positano, Ravello, and Sorrento on a boat trip. I told him that my funds were limited. Flavio responded not to worry about the room, that he would take care of it. After agreeing to see him later in the evening at the Piazzetta for a drink, we parted.

Later, with a smile under his mustache, he appeared at the Caffe Lucio. As I sat in a recessed corner, I was aware that he was well known in Capri and we did not need people to gossip about us. We spent a pleasant hour in each other's company and went separately back to the hotel.

The next day, with my camera and sketchbook, I went down to the docks where I would find the private yacht of Count de Camogli. He was there, jovial, waiting for me. We spent the morning visiting the beautifully appointed yacht. We sipped coffee and ate sweet cakes. The yacht had all modern amenities and a crew of four. I took lots of pictures. Soon Ernesto, his friend and lawyer, arrived and after some more talk and gesticulation, we all left for the restaurant, for a copious lunch of fresh fish, pasta, and a bottle of Chianti. The service was wonderful. The genial host was there! I agreed to meet everyone in the evening for drinks, in the Piazzetta. I returned to my hotel, elated.

The next morning, I made a stop at the Billetteria to inquire about a passage to Amalfi for the next day. A boat was leaving at seven the next morning, so I booked a seat. Returning to the hotel, I saw Flavio at the desk looking sadly at me. I assured him that I would be returning to the hotel after my excursion.

Later, in the Piazzetta, under a full moon, among a crowd of people, I found the table where Maximillan de Camogli and Ernesto were sitting. I was introduced to Adrianna and Roberto, Ernesto's children, handsome young adults. Angela, his wife had high cheek bones and blond hair. The party was animated and cheerful. Since I was to be up at dawn to depart for my trip, I bade farewell to the group and thanked the Count, saying I would paint a picture of his yacht. We all exchanged addresses and I left.

I awoke at dawn, looking through the window to a calm sea and cloudless sky. Packing a few things hastily, I came to the door. Flavio was up and had finished shaving. He asked me to have a cup of coffee in the kitchen. No one else was up yet. We chatted while sipping the strong espresso. He held my hand. I assured him that upon my return, I would stay for two more days before returning to Monaco. This seemed to please him.

The ferry for Sorrento was packed, but I managed to find a seat on deck near the railing. As we docked by the bustling pier, I found Sorrento with its deep blue sea, old stone houses covered with vines, its buildings of yellow ochre and deep pink, lemon trees, and lively piazzas. I spent a couple of hours strolling along the old town. Another boat was to take me to Amalfi. After a slightly choppy ride, we arrived there.

I saw the gleaming white houses built on the rocks, and, at a distance, a church steeple against the jagged mountains of solid boulders. Here and there I spotted trees the color of deep green. The view of Amalfi included its picturesque waterfront with its row of restaurants and cafés, narrow streets leading to the church, and stairs covered with bouquets for a procession. In an old-fashion hotel by the waterfront I found a room for the night. I sketched the next morning, having found interesting scenery by the water.

In the afternoon, I took a bus to the town of Ravello up in the mountains, a small quiet village with curio shops filled with painted ceramic plates. Riding back on the boat, I saw Positano in the distance but did not go ashore. I always like to leave a place for imagination, for the future, for another visit some day.

Back in Capri, Flavio greeted me with his usual big smile. With his slender smallish body, talking with his hands, he looked like a dancer. As I followed him to the kitchen, I saw he was preparing a sauce. Juggling pots and pans, he was graceful in all his gestures. He told me to go to Gino's restaurant and have a good dinner on him. I was expected by the owner. Flavio asked me to meet him later in our usual café on the piazzetta in the evening.

The trattoria was very crowded. The chef, a huge man, greeted me at the door. I ate heartily: minestrone, pasta, fish, wine.

I met Flavio later and thanked him for the wonderful meal. He confided that in a week he was leaving for Pisa to see an allergy doctor. He suggested that I meet him there and we could spend the next four days together, that we would go to Florence. It sounded very romantic to me. I thought of all the museums and works of art. I agreed to meet him in Pisa, but only after telling him that I had to visit my friend Mario Pelletti in Pietrasanta near Carrara. We will go together, he replied. My friend Mario was the celebrated sculptor and great friend of Bufano, my long-time mentor. Flavio's eyes lit up. He seemed so happy and excited, almost dancing, his hand caressed the air. We agreed to speak on the telephone upon my return to Monaco to make our plans.

My last day in Capri was spent sketching the Farraglioni. I made several studies in sepia as I sat in the gardens. After completion, I returned to the hotel to pack my suitcase and paintings. Flavio took me to the boat the next morning. Before I embarked, he gave me a gentle kiss, as people were watching.

Via Napoli, I returned to Rome. On the tiresome train ride to Monte Carlo, I reviewed the last few days. To my surprise, I was excited and anxious at the prospect of returning to Italy in a week to meet a man. As promised, Flavio called me the next day at the home of my friends. He confirmed his arrival in Pisa where he had reserved a room in a hotel for us. I was to leave on the train the next day and await his arrival in the late evening. My friends were curious about this new romance.

The train was direct to Florence but, as Italian trains tend to be, it was late. I was dressed casually and had packed a small bag. I did include in my wardrobe a smart dress, a red suit and a warm rainproof jacket, in addition to casual wear. It was still balmy in Monaco in late fall. I was to return in only a few days. The train was full of backpacking students, but I managed to find a seat in a smoking compartment. After awhile, as the smokers took over the car and its air, I left to stand in the train corridor.

Pisa is a beautiful city. But I was not prepared to see the leaning tower a gleaming white. I had been there briefly in the past and recalled a much darker, pre-cleaned tower. From the station I took a streetcar to the hotel Europa. When I mentioned the name of Signor Cremolini, the man at the desk handed me the key to a room on the second floor. The room was large, with a double bed, and private bath with shower. The small balcony had a view of some cupolas at a distance. I showered and rested on the bed for a couple of hours. By now, it was four in the afternoon and Flavio was not due until eight o'clock that evening.

I took my camera and went out for a walk toward the large piazza at the center of town, toward the tower. Lots of tourists milled around the celebrated site. The sky was clear and blue, and a slight chill was in the air. Luckily, I had my warm jacket. After taking pictures of the tower and viewing the beautiful architecture of the adjacent church, I walked around the square. Souvenir stalls were stuffed with religious mementos, postcards, and the inevitable trinkets. I took everything in stride and returned to the hotel.

In the restaurant, I ordered a snack of proscuitto and melon and went upstairs to the room. It was getting dark. In the air there was a sense of planned intrigue. I turned on my portable radio and Italian love songs filled the room. I sat on the bed thinking of Capri. Presently the telephone rang and it was Flavio. He had arrived at the train station and wanted to make sure that I was all right. I replied that I would be happy to see him.

A slight knock on the door woke me up, as I had dozed off, and Flavio appeared. Trembling, he took me in his arms and kissed me passionately. His lips were soft and a cigarette smell lingered on. He had a voluminous suitcase, which he put atop the dresser and started to unpack. All the while he talked incessantly, excited, half in Italian and half in French. He explained, a riot had started at the station when his train arrived in Pisa. The unruly young crowd was fighting and throwing stones and vandalizing the surroundings. He was angry and frustrated at the delay. We talked of our projects at great length and, exhausted, we both fell asleep. That night on the edge of the bed I again slept badly, not wanting physical contact with Flavio. He had kept his shorts on, and I wore a satin slip.

The next morning, I awoke to find Flavio gone. I heard a knock on the door and he appeared with two cups of espresso and rolls. I got dressed and Flavio and I took the train for Florence, city of arts and beauty. It was raining so we took a taxi to Ponte Vecchio and at one of the shops we purchased an umbrella. In the rain we walked the antique bridges, posing for pictures. I wanted to see the Uffizzi. We paused, admiring the marble statue of David by Michelangelo. The piazza was full of pigeons being fed by small children. The rain had stopped for a while. We passed the Duomo and Basilica. I snapped more pictures. We viewed the bronze gates, the lovely red brick cupolas, and the intricate church architecture. We stopped for a light lunch in a busy caffe. In the afternoon, we stood in line at the Uffizzi and I saw again the Rembrandts, the Botticellis. We walked the long corridors of the museum, mingling with lots of other tourists.

The rain had stopped once again. We strolled on the streets lined with elegant boutiques advertising Armani and Gucci. Smartly-dressed Florentine men and women passed by. We hailed a taxi to the station for our trip back to Pisa. We dined in the hotel restaurant on excellent fish, fried spinach and a custard. Flavio had a glass of spumante.

In the room I noticed how fastidious he was, how meticulous with his clothes. He neatly folded his gray corduroy pants and cashmere sweater atop the drawer. I took a shower and slipped into bed, a bit apprehensive. Soon Flavio stretched next to me and put an arm across my chest. I removed it gently and told him that I was very tired and had a slight headache. His face had a pained look, but he did not insist. I turned on my side and went to sleep.

The next day, on the bus to Montecattini, Flavio explained that he was in the pain of love, aching and frustrated. I replied that I had not promised to give myself to him. That was true, he realized, but he was in love, an Italian man, hot-blooded. He had made this profusely ardent declaration while holding my hand as we sat on the bus. I turned away and admired the verdant valley and hills. We visited the Thermes and the small town. We returned to Pisa via train. I had to take stock of my feelings. No, I did not want an affair. In such a short time I had a certain attraction to Flavio, but I wanted to keep the feeling of romance. That night after cautious words of endearment, I explained to Flavio that I needed more time to get to know him. I slept chastely in his arms, listening to his breathing.

In the morning, while sipping our coffee, I told Flavio about a friend of mine living in Pietrasanta. I had mentioned him previously. Excited to please me, he acquiesced to take the trip. We arrived in pouring rain at the station. I had Mario Pelletti's number so I ran in the wet street to a café to telephone him. He was surprised and excited to see me again. We arrived at Mario's studio. After the presentations, Mario showed us his sculptures. Taking pictures, I spotted a small white marble owl sculpted by Bufano, Mario's dear friend. He was reluctant to part with it, but I slipped a thousand franc note in his hand. I knew that in the end, he would give it to me. He showed us more works by Bufano including some drawings and a small Saint Francis statue in bronze, that Mario obviously cherished. He took us to Fonderia Mariani where we saw gigantic Botero sculptures cast in bronze. We thanked Mario profusely and promised to write.

After leaving Pietrasanta, as it was still early, we decided to take a train for Lucca, truly a charming Italian city with a circular piazza and pastel houses. We strolled this medieval town, browsing in the shops. Flavio was carrying my purchases. We stopped briefly for a quick lunch at a sidewalk café. The weather was cool and sunny. It was our last day together.

On the train, Flavio was silent. I took his hand and pressed it to my bosom. Looking into his eyes I said that this was a wonderful trip, that I enjoyed everything immensely and that I was sad it would end. Flavio suddenly became animated and talked haltingly. He related that every year for two months he left his family to go to Rio de Janeiro on vacation. He would like to take me there. Plans were forming in his head, his eyes sparkling, his hands flying in the air. Would I come? We could meet in San Francisco, my home. How very romantic, I thought, seeing myself with Flavio, dancing to the exciting beat of sambas in one of the night clubs of Rio. I loved Rio and told him so, never having been there at Carnival time. Then we would go in January and February, he insisted.

Returning to our hotel to pack, we kissed, holding each other. I saw a tear in his eye and I felt a knot in my throat. Flavio's plane to Rome was at noon, but my train was not until eight o'clock. Flavio had paid the hotel bill and told me to have dinner, that it was taken care of. How considerate of him. He was to call me in a few days in Monte Carlo at my friend's home. On the return trip I was dreaming of my romance and the trip to Rio with a romantic Italian. I was building up a big dream. I promised to myself to have a passionate love affair, something to remember forever.

I never got his call. Flavio was killed when his airplane crashed, while trying to land in the fog near Rome.

Epilogue

After Carl's death in the spring of 1988, I had to take stock of my life and reorganize my priorities in my work and family life. During my last year in Monaco, I had one more art exhibit at the Hotel de Paris, which was received very well. I sold many paintings in 1989 and after that July show I decided to move back to San Francisco. Gregg and Kitt had a son Brad, now a year and a half old. They were expecting their second child.

I found a charming flat with a garden in the back and with a large, sunny room for my studio. It was the day I moved into this new home, in the fall of 1989, that the earth shook in San Francisco, the Loma Prieta quake. Part of my old district, the Marina, was in flames with collapsed buildings and buckled sidewalks. My new flat was near Golden Gate Park. I enjoyed the salubrious walks every morning.

Gregg and Kitt were living in southern California with their son, Brad, and their new daughter, Kathy. I visited them often and played with the children, whom I loved without measure. In 1990, they moved back to the Bay Area and I was overjoyed to see them more often. Gregg bought a large home and set up his business near Sacramento. I was organizing art exhibits in hotels and restaurants in San Francisco. The sale of my paintings and watercolors were brisk.

In the late fall of 1991, I went to France, to visit my brother Andy, his wife Ingrid, and their daughters. I spent a week in Paris where I returned to the same old haunts: St Germain, Montparnasse and the Latin Quarter. Things had changed but I could always find a place that was reminiscent of my past. I visited my friend Lyvia, who was well, and saw her new apartment in Paris.

On the plane home, an ominous impulse overtook me to use the airphone to call Gregg. I was always thinking of him and the children, but logic prevailed. It was foolish to call as I was to see them soon. I put the thought in the back of my mind. The plane arrived in the late evening from Paris and I was tired when I arrived at my flat in San Francisco.

The month in France had exhausted me, emotionally and physically. I decided to wait to call Gregg the next morning, as was my custom. What happened next was a nightmare. Gregg's voice did not have the same cheerful tone. I did not question him too much as he said he was coming to the city for a business appointment and would see me.

When I opened the door to let him in, I found an ashen-faced Gregg. I cried, "What happened?" Gregg said in a low voice, "We lost Kathy." I screamed at the top of my voice, "No. No!" A hundred screams of no went through my psyche. I ran, like a fool, to the neighbor's arms and sobbed uncontrollably. Poor Gregg. I realized I had left him standing alone in my home. My son, who had just lost his precious little girl. It had been a horrible accident. The baby had been strangled by the strings on her dress, as she was trying to climb out of her crib. No one was to blame. I told Gregg to lie on the sofa and, though shaken, I made him some hot tea. Tearing at my clothes, I cried and hugged my son. We then returned to his home, as the funeral was to be the next day. I called my friend Bianca, who was always there for me.

The next few days were a nightmare. All I remember was Gregg and Kitt at the church, leaning on each other. The little white coffin was open but I could not bear to see her, my precious little Kathy. I asked Bianca to see her for me. I always will remember her pearly teeth, her soft warm body after her bath, when I put talcum powder on her. How she giggled. How I always patted her little tummy. Oh, God, it is so difficult even eight years after her death. Her brief time in this life was only twenty short months. She is with the Lord now. Bless her soul. Life will never be the same. I thought that losing my mother, father, and brother in the Holocaust was so horrible. I never thought that a greater tragedy would touch my life. I was wrong! So wrong!

Life continued. I cherished my little grandson Brad. Kitt and Gregg were disconsolate that first year, but their strong faith and desire to have another child prevailed. After many months of trying, Kitt could not conceive. We prayed together at church. Coming home, I would hold myself while sitting in the bathtub and cry bitterly all the tears of my body. Sobbing, sobbing. The tears fell into the water. That was when I decided after many months to take a pen in hand to write, as a form of therapy, about my past, beginning as a small child in Paris. This decision forced me to go back in years, recounting the past and not thinking of the present, of this tragic loss of this precious child.

The time passed and my memoirs were taking shape. On my trip to France that summer of 1994, I went to Lourdes and prayed on my knees to the Madonna for a blessing. Lourdes was a great experience. I walked in the throng of chanting people to the grotto where the miracle of the sight of the Virgin appeared to Bernadette, a young village girl. I felt propelled by a singular force and felt as if I was levitating. The people were carrying small candles through the grotto. I lit some candles and prayed all night.

That Christmas, I took Gregg and his family to Hawaii. We spent a warm holiday together in Honolulu at a hotel by the ocean. We returned home refreshed. In the middle of January 1995, Kitt announced she was pregnant. What joy! We were ecstatic and thanked the Lord for this miracle. In September, she delivered a tiny adorable baby girl. They named her Beth. I was so thrilled and spent as much time as possible with them. Little Beth looked so like our precious Kathy. Blessed be the name of the Lord!

I was still painting, but my eyes were giving me problems. That year I was diagnosed with retinal cancer. Terribly frightened, I sought treatment in Paris, but the Hospital Currie sent me to Boston. There, I underwent an operation, followed by a series of radiation treatments. I was devastated but so grateful that the doctors were able to save my eye, although I couldn't be certain that I was totally rid of the cancer.

I was a month in Boston. I prayed a lot and listened to Christian broadcasts on the radio every night. I felt so alone. It was a terrible ordeal but I found that the Lord had in fact opened my eyes to a spiritual life. From then on, I was trying to be a child of God and I took Jesus into my life and accepted him as my savior. I read the bible and attended Sunday church services with my son and his family. We prayed together, something I had never done in the past. I prayed that my sins would be forgiven.

I knew somehow that I had been saved from the Holocaust, that God in his infinite mercy intended for me to survive, to live. As the Bible says, "In life you will have tribulation." But to overcome and to be at peace is very difficult. However, I did the best I could, resuming my life, painting and having several exhibits in hotels in San Francisco.

On New Year's eve of 1997, I underwent a second operation on my right cheek to remove a melanoma the doctors had discovered. A portion of my neck was lifted to cover my cheek as a large patch of tissue was removed. It changed my appearance and for many months I felt disfigured. But the necessity to remove the tumor was a priority. I was hopeful to have reconstructive surgery in the future.

Gregg and Kitt had strong faith and worshipped the Lord in every way they could. They were in a group of devoted young people in their church.

Gregg was a leader in Sunday school and Kitt did much volunteer work at church. The children were thriving and it was my great happiness to spend time with Gregg and his family.

Also that summer found me again as a lecturer on a cruise ship for a twelve-day Mediterranean voyage. We went to Spain, Portugal, Italy, and France. I lectured on history, economy, art, and architecture. It was most enjoyable. I left the ship, which had been renamed *Norway*, but it was, in truth, the old venerable *France*, refurbished and one of the largest cruise ships afloat of the Norwegian cruise line.

Returning home, I resumed painting with new energy and did in the impressionistic style some large, colorful canvasses of the south of France and of ladies with large hats in languid poses. The canvasses were on exhibit in a gallery in Carmel. I had achieved some sort of professional status. I alternated my painting with writing surges. It has been ten years now that I have lived in my flat in San Francisco.

Recently, I received a letter that intrigued me greatly from an old friend of mine who still lived in Paris. He was one of the hidden children saved from the Holocaust who shared my life briefly in Malmaison during the postwar years. He wrote that a Swedish man was looking for me, that I was his mother's cousin. The man's name was Jens Karlberg, and he had been trying to find me and my brother. During his research in archives in France, he had not found our names on lists of Holocaust martyrs. In desperation, he put a small ad in a Paris paper, asking our whereabouts. One day he got the answers from my old friend, who remembered me from the orphanage of Malmaison, and who told him I was in America. I wrote, asking Jens Karlberg for more information. In response, I received a letter telling me that my mother's niece, my first cousin, was alive and had three sons living in Sweden with their families. Jens was the youngest son.

By some miracle, my cousin, my mother Lola's niece Terenia, was saved as a young woman from the burning Warsaw ghetto during the time of the Nazis. My mother was from Poland and I had not ever heard of any of her relatives surviving after Krystallnacht, as the Germans entered Poland first. I knew that some of my father's cousins were living in England, as I had found them on my first visit back to Europe, years before. I always visited them upon my trips to Europe. But on my mother's side, no one, until now. It had taken Jens fifty years to find me and my brother Andy. As neither of us were on the list of the victims of the Holocaust, Jens knew a chance existed that we had survived. Because we were the "Hidden Children." Survivors!

Great was my emotion when I spoke to my cousin Jens over the telephone. My cousin Terenia, my mother's niece, now an aged lady, spoke French to me across the miles and across time. Andy went to visit them in Stockholm and was received warmly. Our other cousin Krista still lives in Warsaw and has a daughter in the United States. So, the miracle goes on!

God has allowed me to have a new family, that of my dear mother. With my family, Gregg, Kitt, and their children Brad, ten, and Beth, four, we went to France in the summer of 1999, for the wedding of Andy and Ingrid's youngest daughter, Anya. A new beginning, in so many ways. From two surviving orphans, our family now numbers more than fifty.

Blessed be the Lord. I am grateful that I can look with serenity at my past and hope that God will forgive my sins. I pray for the best in the new century. Whatever it brings, I only ask for health and peace. As Bufano would say, "Peace be with you."